MARK

IN THE LECTIONARY

MARK

IN THE LECTIONARY

*An Ecumenical Guide
to the Sunday Gospels*

Gérald Caron

Paulist Press
New York/Mahwah, NJ

Library of Congress Cataloging-in-Publication Data

Caron, Gérald.
    Mark in the lectionary : an ecumenical guide to the Sunday Gospels / Gérald Caron.
        p. cm.
    ISBN 978-0-8091-4591-1 (alk. paper)
    1. Bible. N.T. Mark--Textbooks. 2. Catholic Church. Lectionary for Mass (U.S.) I. Title.
    BS2586.C37 2008
    226.3'06--dc22

                                        2008025792

Published by Paulist Press
997 Macarthur Boulevard
Mahwah, New Jersey 07430

www.paulistpress.com

Printed and bound in the
United States of America

*To my students
Atlantic School of Theology
(1988–2005)*

Contents

PREFACE

In some sense, this book is the result of my last twenty years of teaching the Gospel of Mark at the Atlantic School of Theology in Halifax, Nova Scotia. Not only was Mark the first gospel I taught but, together with John, quickly became one of my favorite gospels. Building upon an ever-growing interaction with my students, it also became the launching pad for developing a new interactive approach or methodology for teaching the gospels. It is this approach, which has proved pedagogically effective, that has made its way into this study guide.

Because of the demands and expectations that this approach made on students, their contribution to its development and fine-tuning was major and valuable. I owe much to them and, to show my appreciation, dedicate this study guide to them. Second, I am also indebted to the works of many scholars with whom I have interacted over the years in my own work on the Gospel of Mark. The few occasional references to some of their works owe more to the restrictions imposed by the genre of this book than by the lack of recognition that they would rightly deserve. Finally, I want to express my heartfelt gratitude to Margaret Lake, MDiv., for her valuable contribution to the final edition of this book. She was not only a great help in the tedious work of refining my English grammar and style but, thanks to her insightful comments and theological savvy, also has contributed to reformulating some of my own theological thoughts. Without her gracious help, this book would be different.

INTRODUCTION

This book has a twofold objective. It is a pedagogical tool (study guide) for preachers as well as those engaging in Bible study groups. It is also a contemporary presentation of Mark, and it will examine questions raised in the contexts of today.

A different book

As a study guide on the Sunday Gospel and First Testament readings, this is primarily a teaching tool for preachers and readers of the Bible. It may, for some, call for thorough and sustained work. It will engage and sometimes challenge readers on many levels. I believe that both preachers and readers of the Bible will greatly benefit from their efforts and discover a renewed enthusiasm towards the Word of God. Congregations too will benefit greatly from this renewed enthusiasm as preachers and readers become more deeply engaged with the Word of God.

A postmodern approach

Before setting this pedagogical tool in motion, let me say a word about the second objective of this book. My approach to the biblical text of Mark is inspired by what I would call a postmodern consciousness.

Giving the reader a voice. I am aware that the very word "postmodern" may evoke skepticism and suspicion because the term is often associated with deconstruction, relativism, and fragmentation. When applied to the biblical text, however, the postmodern stance invites readers to join with the text in the search for truths. Such an approach is based on the conviction that today's reader plays an active role in the interpretation of a biblical text. It is not enough to know about the historical context, which produced a given text, or to learn about what the historical writers meant to say, or, more simply what the text was meant to convey. For any real interpretation to take place, the reader must enter into conversation with the passage. Only such interaction between text and readers—today's readers with all their cultural and social differences—will ultimately bring about an ethical or responsible interpretation. This conversation between readers and text is primarily what this book encourages.

Not so new an approach. This approach is not as new as one may think. It's already being used in our Churches. One of many examples is the text of Ephesians 5:21–32, once the official passage for wedding days in many of our Churches. Because Christian women and men of today no longer understand their marriage relationships in the terms described in this passage, it is now generally not used in North America as well as in Europe. In other words, this new perception of marital relationships has couples "authorizing themselves" to replace this once important text with a "word" more fitting and relevant to their understanding of marriage.

Contextualized reading. Although it is attached to Mark, the term "postmodern" does not make the evangelist into a postmodern before his time. The term applies to today's readers of Mark. The majority of readers today, consciously or not, will not read Mark's Gospel independently of their cultural, political, social, and religious context. For example, a Catholic reader or preacher of the Markan text on divorce (10:1–12) may be hard pressed not to think of the difficulties that so many divorced people endure because of their Church directive concerning intimate relationships after divorce. If divorced persons engage in intimate relationship, their Church communities no longer welcome them at the Eucharistic Table. This painful situation will prompt readers or preachers to pay attention to this biblical passage and its "reception history." There are many ways of interpreting our Scripture texts. I believe a postmodern perspective will provide a more ethically and morally responsible interpretation for people of today.

Post-Holocaust reading. Examples such as the one provided above could be multiplied and readers will, in fact, find several more in this study guide. One such example will be given special attention, the delicate question of anti-Judaism in Mark's Gospel. Scholarly treatments of this question have generally paid little attention to the Gospel of Mark. Yet, there is a growing awareness of the fact that some texts may promote and perpetuate Christian anti-Judaism. This awareness has drastically changed the way many of us are now reading passages that, until recently, appeared to be no cause for alarm. This new sensitivity results from the Holocaust (*Shoah*) and the hard reflections it has fostered among Christians of all persuasion. The acceptance that Christianity's influential teaching of contempt towards Judaism and the Jewish people was a contributing factor in this horrific tragedy has caused all mainline Churches to reflect and act. They have responded to the challenge of transforming this age-old teaching of contempt into a teaching of respect. To that effect, these Churches have produced important documents on this question, not only rejecting the teaching of contempt in all its manifestations, but urging their members and constituencies to be aware of contemptuous teachings in their liturgical texts, books, sermons, and Catechesis. All members and constituencies are urged to address anything that might be disparaging of Jews and their institutions. In the Roman Catholic Church alone, the great insights of the Vatican II declaration *Nostra Aetate* (n. 4) have been implemented over the past 40 years in some important documents from Rome and countless other statements from local and national Churches. Given the sad history of Christian anti-Semitism and the ever present danger that some Christian texts may still cultivate feelings of hatred towards Jews, mainline Churches, teachers and preachers in particular, face the colossal task of reversing a teaching that has now been officially rejected and condemned. This book will, through questions and the occasional reflection, try to also raise awareness of this important issue.

The use of First Testament and Second Testament instead of Old Testament and New Testament has been adopted to avoid any theology of supersessionism. Supersession, which regards Judaism as not merely having been supplanted by Christianity, but that the covenant between God and Israel as his chosen people has been abrogated, was a prevalent heresy now condemned by quite nearly all Christian denominations. That kind of prevalent view was a factor in numerous programs throughout the ages that culminated in the Holocaust.

In the same way BCE (Before the Current Era) and CE (Current Era) are used instead of BC (Before Christ) and AD (Anno Domini or Year of the Lord) in order to show we are sensitive to our Jewish brothers and sisters and to avoid even a hint of anti-Semitism.

A PEDAGOGICAL TOOL

To help readers become familiar with the process, the same pattern will be used throughout this book. Each brief chapter will include a short analysis of the reading from the First Testament, followed by a more complex analysis of the assigned Markan passages. Narrative analysis will be employed as a methodology in the interpretation of the Markan passages. Questions will follow, then interpretive points, and finally some pastoral and homiletical notes.

The choice of the First Testament reading in the *Roman Catholic Lectionary* is clearly intended to connect with the Gospel text of the day. As a general rule, it was selected to root what the Gospel text proclaims about Christ in the Jewish tradition. Yet, in ascribing a christological meaning to the First Testament text, such juxtaposition has the potential to create a supersessionist view. This potential to *replace* the First Testament or Judaism by the Second Testament or Christianity is something that all Churches are now committed to eradicate from their teaching. As was made clear in the 2002 document from the Biblical Commission, *The Jewish People and their Scriptures in the Christian Bible*, Christian reading of First Testament texts in no way invalidates the Jewish reading of these same texts. It is to offset both this danger and to address what now are seen as tenuous connections between First and Second Testament texts that the *Revised Common Lectionary* offers an alternative First Testament reading. Our pastoral and homiletical notes will, whenever it is deemed necessary, point out the risks involved in ignoring the potential for supersessionism.

Now, a brief explanation of the four stages of our pedagogical process.

Narrative context: Many years of teaching experience have taught me that context, the narrative context in particular, is not given the attention it deserves in the interpretive process. As an integral part of the narrative from which it draws its meaning, the passage or pericope feeds, so to speak, on the narrative context. Although such contexts will be provided, mainly to save time for your analysis, they should not preclude your reading of Mark's narrative. To those who might point to the absence of such contexts from the Lectionary readings and their importance, I can only point out to the usual introduction given before the passage is read, "A reading from . . . the Gospel of Mark." This introduction should remind congregations that the little snippet of text that they are about to listen to is part of and drawn from a much larger narrative, the Gospel itself.

Questions. This second stage constitutes the heart of the interpretive exercise and will, no doubt, offer the greatest challenge. Two sets of three or four questions will be provided. While still demanding some research, the first set are more of a general type and perhaps more adaptable for Bible study groups. The second set will generally require more analysis, reflection, and sensitivity to contemporary issues. The primary purpose of the questions provided is to help "open up" the text. They do not, and in fact cannot, exhaust the full range of meaning of the text. I have learned over the years how difficult it is to formulate questions. Questions are never entirely neutral; although they carry, of necessity, the interests of those who formulate them, they should not be too overtly leading in one particular direction. I have worked with this awareness and struggled to formulate questions that will challenge readers on many different levels.

Interpretive points. This section does not provide a running commentary on the Gospel text. Rather, it provides analytical input on the questions, often in the form of flashbacks to elements of the text already covered in your analysis that may require clarification. Occasionally, comments will also be provided on various issues related to, or raised by, a given passage or the Gospel narrative at large (e.g., Mark's use of Scripture quotations and their legitimating function in the narrative, typical features like his favorite "sandwich technique" or the so-called messianic secret, theological and ethical issues around miracles, marriage and divorce, textual and translation problems, and many more). These and similar issues will affect the way one will understand and interpret the biblical text.

Pastoral and homiletical notes. It is my intention in this final section to provide comments, thematic connections, and occasional reflections as resources for preachers and readers. It is not my intention to submit outlines, still less samples, of sermons or Bible studies. You are the preachers and teachers! It is my hope that both preachers and readers will dialogue with these texts and relate them to contemporary issues that are relevant to our congregations and to society at large. In conclusion, it is also my hope that this study guide will help you develop an approach to biblical texts that will lead to a more extensive and deeper ethical awareness of the responsibility involved in interpreting, teaching, and preaching these texts.

Advent Season

The season of Advent begins the liturgical year of the Church. It is a time of preparation for the Christian celebration of God's incarnation, or manifestation, in Jesus of Nazareth at Christmas. Yet, it is quite remarkable that Christians are invited, on the first Sunday of Advent, to look beyond Jesus' coming into this world to the Second coming of Christ. It is from this perspective that Christians are to understand what is about to be proclaimed and celebrated at Christmas. The liturgy of the following Sundays moves to the more traditional structure provided by the first three Gospels. On the second Sunday, congregations will hear one Synoptic version of the prophetic call and ministry of John the Baptist, while this same John, seen through the eyes of the Fourth evangelist, will reappear in the Gospel reading of the following Sunday. The Advent period concludes, on the fourth Sunday, with the reading of Luke's annunciation story (1:26–38).

In the year of Mark, the only texts to be heard from the Gospel of Mark during Advent will be read on the first (13:33–37) and second (1:1–8) Sunday.

1. First Sunday of Advent

Year B

Roman Catholic L
Isaiah 63:16b–17; 64:1, 3–8
Mark 13:33–37

Revised Common L
Isaiah 64:1–9
Mark 13:24–37

Trust God and Learn to Watch
(Mark 13:33–37)

On Isaiah 63:16b–17; 64:1, 3–8

The "great vision" of the second part of the book (chapters 40—55) had yet to be fulfilled when today's reading was composed. Generally believed to come from post-exilic times, the last section of the book of Isaiah 56—66 reflects, in part, some of the frustrations and tensions of that period. The selection of today, chosen from this last section, is part of a larger psalm of lament (63:7—64:11). Like all biblical laments, it ultimately is a confident cry to God for help in times of need.

The people's plea for God's saving intervention is at the center of today's passage: "O that you would tear open the heavens and come down" (64:1)! It is sandwiched between two descriptions of the people's distress and their sense of loss over God's anger and abandonment (63:17–19 and 64:5–7). Notwithstanding the hint that God may in some way be responsible for their transgressions and sins (64:7), the people go on to rehearse the same bold statement of trust and confidence made at the outset (63:16). They again address their Lord as "Father" (64:8), pleading to, once more, tear open the heavens and come down to save them.

9

ON MARK 13:33–37
Context

Today's Gospel reading is the conclusion to a lengthy discourse of Mark 13. It is sometimes called the "Little Apocalypse" because it uses apocalyptic language and imagery of the end time to speak of hope, courage, and endurance to a community seemingly under persecution. The chapter comes somewhat as a surprise, interrupting the narrative flow. Jesus' confrontation with the authorities in Mark 11—12 would seemingly be a more suitable preparation for the final confrontation about to take place in the passion (Mark 14—15). This Little Apocalypse compels readers to pause, bringing them to a halt in order for them to listen to Jesus. He is addressing "in private" the first disciples that he has called to follow him (1:16–20).

Through the words of Jesus, Mark is addressing a community going through difficult times during the dramatic events of the first Jewish rebellion which ends in the destruction of both Jerusalem and its Temple in 70 CE (vv. 9–13 and 14–20). He then goes on to warn the community not to be led astray by false interpretations or readings of "these things" (vv. 21–23). To those who stay alert and show perseverance to the end, vindication will come when, after some further cosmic disruption, the Son of Man returns with great power and glory to gather the elect (vv. 26–27). Immediately preceding today's selection is a warning that no one but God knows the day or the hour of this return (vv. 28–32). In today's reading, this Little Apocalypse discourse ends with a final exhortation to be on the watch (vv. 33–37).

Questions

1. Can you detect words or expressions that unify, both rhetorically and thematically, these concluding verses of the Little Apocalypse?
2. How does the parable in verse 34 help define what it means to be watchful or vigilant?
3. What do you think of Jesus' very last word (v. 37) before entering the passion?

✦ ✦ ✦

4. From your reading of Mark 13, can you figure out what the "disciples" are expected to do while their master is absent?

5. What might be the purpose of placing this extended discourse of Jesus in Mark 13 immediately before the passion narrative?

6. What do you think of using a text referring to the second coming to prepare a celebration of the historical first coming of Christ at Christmas?

Interpretive points

1. *Reading in context.* To fully understand the thrust of Jesus' final exhortation to be watchful, readers will need to acquaint themselves with chapter 13 of Mark in its entirety. More specifically, today's reading should be read in its narrative context, verses 24–32, which forms part of the *Revised Common Lectionary*'s selection for this Sunday.

2. *On Mark 13.* For brief remarks on the apocalyptic genre and the Little Apocalypse of Mark 13, see the Thirty-Third Sunday in Ordinary Time/Proper 28.

3. *Watching, staying awake, and alert.* Although a different Greek word is used in verse 33, the idea of watching or staying awake (the opposite of "falling asleep" in v. 36) undergirds this final unit of the discourse (vv. 35 and 37).

4. *Learning to become "servants."* Both here and throughout the chapter, the little parable of verse 34 is key to understanding what Jesus' frequent call to vigilance means. When read as an allegory of life in the community, it depicts followers of Christ as those "servants" who, with their master traveling abroad, are left in charge, each with work to be done. The work entrusted to them and for which they have been granted power is to proclaim the Good News to all nations (v. 10). Such proclamation will, of necessity, as for Jesus, encounter opposition, persecution, and even death. When these events occur, they should be seen not as "signs" of the approaching end time but, rather, as the outcome of the power struggle that Jesus has initiated with the powers of Evil. It is to this same struggle that he summons his disciples.

5. *"What I say to you, I say to all: Keep awake" (v. 37).* By locating this chapter immediately before the passion narrative, Mark informs his

readers that their upcoming story can only be understood in light of what happens to both Jesus and the disciples in the following chapters. The community and readers are warned to "keep awake," like "servants" waiting for their Master to return. They will be facing "situations," perhaps they already do, similar to those that Jesus and the disciples are about to face in the passion. Will they, like Jesus, be found watching, awake, faithful to the end, or like the male disciples, sleepy, uncertain, and frightened?

Pastoral and homiletical notes

1. *Changing context.* By separating today's exhortation from its immediate context (vv. 28–32), the *Roman Catholic Lectionary* makes it more difficult for preachers and hearers to grasp the thrust of Jesus' final words. On the other hand, this hermeneutical move makes it easier for preachers to apply words, originally geared towards the second coming, to the context of Advent and preparation for the first coming of Christ at Christmas. Still, however difficult the task may be, in order to remain true to the Gospel, preachers may want to address this issue.

2. *Introducing the cycle of Mark's Gospel.* Mark 13:33–37 is the first text to be heard from Mark in the year B cycle. Whether the time is right or not for some introductory words about this Gospel is up to preachers, but a word of information about moving into the cycle of Mark's Gospel may be appropriate at this point.

3. *A key parable.* If the interpretation given above is correct, the little parable offers preachers the best insight into what Jesus' exhortation to be vigilant, watchful, or alert is all about. In Advent, the Church invites all its members to be vigilant, watchful, and alert as they prepare for the upcoming celebration of the coming of Christ at Christmas. As the title of the late Raymond E. Brown's booklet suggested, *Bringing Christ Back into Christmas,* there is more to Christmas than simply celebrating or remembering the historical birth of Jesus. In a real sense, without the eschatological dimension of the early Church's proclamation of the second coming, there would be little to cele-

brate at Christmas. Advent time is about preparing for a better understanding of God's incarnation into our world. To be vigilant, watchful, or alert is to be, now and at all times, like the servants of the parable, to bear witness to the good news around us.

4. *Tearing open the heavens!* "O that you would tear open the heavens and come down to show your face to us" (Isa 64:1). Might this be the attitude expected from Christians today as they prepare in hopeful prayer for God's decisive appearance in the person of Jesus, the Christ at Christmas?

2. SECOND SUNDAY OF ADVENT
Year B

Roman Catholic L   *Revised Common L*
Isaiah 40:1–5, 9–11   Isaiah 40:1–11
Mark 1:1–8   Mark 1:1–8

LEGITIMATING JOHN THE BAPTIST:
THE FORERUNNER OF JESUS
(MARK 1:1–8)

ON ISAIAH 40:1–11

This passage from Isaiah opens a section of the book generally attributed to an unknown prophet from the exilic period. It proclaims that things are about to change for the people. Their harsh judgment is over, and their salvation has come. What is now in shambles will be reconstructed. They must, therefore, be comforted because God is coming with might (v. 10). Make sure that a way is prepared in the wilderness for his return because the Lord will feed his flock like a shepherd (v. 11). Although such a vision of things will certainly have discomforting implications for whoever is called upon to announce these good tidings, they must not fear to speak out against the flimsy Empire, God is coming (vv. 6–8)!

ON MARK 1:1–8
Context

The first 13 or 15 verses of Mark have variously been called a prologue, a preface, an introduction, or simply the beginning of the Gospel. There is no consensus among scholars as to where this "introduction" ends, in verse 13 or verse 15. More surprisingly, it is not even clear where it actually begins, in verse 1 or in verse 2. The answer to this last question will depend on how one finally reads the first line of Mark: as a reference to the ministry of John the Baptist (a simple chronological reference) or as a title or superscription for the whole Gospel?

Questions

1. How do you read Mark 1:1, as the title for the whole Gospel or as its chronological beginning? What meaning would you ascribe to the initial words "the beginning" in either reading?
2. What do you think is the narrative and rhetorical function of the "Isaian" citation in verses 2–3?
3. What is so important about John's dress and eating habits that they need to be mentioned?

4. Do you think it is relevant for Christians today to know that the Qumran community also used the same passage from Isaiah (therefore prior to Mark) to ground their own wilderness experience?
5. Why would some translations (such as *The Good News Bible*) alter Mark's indication in verse 5 that *all of* Judea and Jerusalem flock to John to be baptized and confess their sins?
6. What do you think is the narrative function of John's testimony in verses 7–8?

Interpretive points

1. *Textual problem.* Should the title "Son of God" be part of or omitted from the text of Mark 1:1? The manuscript tradition is almost equally divided here, with "Son of God" appearing in some and not appearing in others. Textual critics are hard pressed to suggest what the "original text" might have looked like. Some bible translations, like the NRSV and NAB, will bracket the title in the text while others will include it with a footnote attached. Others will simply omit it. Readers should be alerted to this textual problem because of its possible theological impact on the whole Gospel.

2. *Reading Isaiah Christologically.* The quotation from Isaiah in Mark 1:3 follows very closely the Greek text—often referred to as the Septuagint (LXX). A quick comparison of Mark's version with the passage of Isa-

iah in your Bible will show a sharp difference between the two versions. Why? Mark, like most of the evangelists, quotes from the Greek text, not the Hebrew text (Isa 40:3) that would not have been useful to Mark's purpose. As you must have discovered (if you have answered question 3 above), Mark goes further. Not only has he combined the text of Isaiah with one from Malachi (and possibly also with a reference from the book of Exodus), but has also altered some of the pronouns, to ensure that the text would now apply to Jesus. This sort of manipulation may be disturbing, even bewildering for some of us, yet, such manipulation is common in the Gospels as well as in the rest of the Second Testament. These strategies, for this is what they really are, contribute to a Christian or Christological reading of the First Testament/Jewish Scriptures. Remember: The Gospels are very much rhetorical writings, and Mark is no different from the others. As the "title" already implies, Mark's purpose in writing his Gospel is to persuade people that Jesus is the Christ and the Son of God (1:1).

3. *Inside information.* Readers of Mark 1:1–13 are given a large amount of "inside" information about Jesus. All this information—unavailable to the characters of the narrative—is intended to help the reader to follow along and accept the various claims that are made throughout the story about Jesus. In this respect, these verses are a key for understanding the rest of the Gospel. To fully understand the information provided here, readers have, however, no alternative but to continue reading.

4. *What beginning?* Whatever your answer to the first question was, it is only when verse 1 is taken as a title that what the word "beginning" might refer to requires attention. If only the beginning of the Good News of Jesus, Christ, Son of God, is found in the actual text of Mark, where then is the rest? Could it be in the history of the Church? The prospect is fascinating: The Gospel of Jesus, Christ and Son of God, beginning in Mark, is proclaimed today but continues to unfold.

Pastoral and homiletical notes

1. *Christian reading.* In applying the words of Isaiah 40:3 (and Mal 3:1) to John the Baptist, Mark reads the text in terms of the coming (ad-

vent) of Christ at Christmas. John is now the voice crying in the wilderness, preparing the way for the stronger one who is coming after him. Likewise, through its selection of the Isaian passage for the Second Sunday of Advent, the Church confirms the Christological reading that Mark has already made of a First Testament text.

2. *Claims and strategies.* Advent preparation for the Christmas celebration of God's appearance among us in Jesus is as good a context as any for preachers to reflect on the extraordinary faith claims that are made in this Gospel passage, and the strategies used to convey them. For example, Mark uses Scriptural texts—even modifying them—to carry his message about John the Baptist and Jesus. As your own research will have shown, he also makes use of the well-known typological approach—dressing John in Malachi's garb—to transform the Baptist into the eschatological prophet announced in this last prophetic book.

3. *All about faith claims.* Preachers would do well to remember that all four Gospels—Mark included—use (their) Scripture to legitimate (authenticate) the claims they make about Jesus or the claims they have Jesus make about God and about himself. In the above comments, the term "legitimate" was used, not randomly, but to draw attention to what is in fact happening in the text. In today's multicultural, pluralistic, and largely secular world, the world in which Christians are called to live, our congregations must be informed that what is said or implied of John here (and later of Jesus) is as good as the books on which these very claims are based. In the end, what it comes to is all a matter of faith and, I would like to suggest, there is no better preparation for the Christmas celebration than to stress this very fact for all to hear.

4. *Catechesis in Advent.* Preachers could also use the same context of Advent to discuss the many lenses through which Scriptures can be viewed, as well as to foster respect for how different faith communities may interpret the same scriptural text.

CHRISTMAS AND EPIPHANY

Without an Infancy or Birth narrative, no passage from Mark's Gospel makes the Christmas and Epiphany season. Mark has nothing to say about the conception, birth, and early years of Jesus as found in Matthew and Luke or, as proclaimed in the Johannine prologue (1:1–18) about the incarnation of the Word!

The absence of a Birth narrative in Mark should not cause the Gospel to be viewed as incomplete or less significant. If anything, such particularity teaches something that might be worth pondering at Christmas time. Writing around 70 CE, this evangelist has produced a full-fledged Gospel, without saying a word concerning the "miraculous" events surrounding the conception and birth of Jesus. It should also be recalled that Mark's Gospel lacks any appearance stories of the risen Jesus! These stories were either not yet available to him (or Paul), or if any were, the evangelist did not consider that they added anything theologically relevant to what is already clearly stated at the start of his Gospel: The beginning of the Good News of Jesus, Christ, Son of God (v. 1). Mark's lack of an Infancy or Birth narrative may teach readers and preachers how to read the Christmas texts from Matthew and Luke's Infancy Narratives from a completely new perspective.

3. Baptism of the Lord
Year B

Roman Catholic L   ***Revised Common L***

Isaiah 55:1–11   Genesis 1:1–5

Mark 1:7–11   Mark 1:4–11

YOU ARE MY SON, THE BELOVED
(MARK 1:7–11)

ON ISAIAH 55:1–11

Today's selection, from the book of Isaiah, is the conclusion of what is often referred to as the Book of Consolation (Isa 40—55), generally attributed to an unknown prophet from the exilic period. It concludes with an (last) appeal to heed the Lord's words about Israel's future restoration (55:1–13). This strong appeal to faith in the fulfillment of God's word may well speak to the difficulties these people will encounter as they return to face a destroyed temple and a devastated homeland.

The passage can be divided into three parts. The first part (vv. 1–5) begins with an invitation, coined in the language of Lady Wisdom (Pr 9:4–8), to approach the table of the Lord (vv. 1–3a). The food of this table is nothing less than the Lord's everlasting covenant with the entire nation. They, as David once was, will now be called to witness to all nations (vv. 3b–5). In the second part (vv. 6–11), the people are invited to put their trust in the Lord and fully accept the Lord's ways—God's plan of salvation for them. Incomprehensible though this plan may be at the present time (think of the mysterious activity of the suffering servant in chapters 52—53), Israel is now called to accept that the Lord's word is reliable and effective. When the Lord speaks, things happen! The third and last part (vv. 12–13), which has been omitted from the lection, rehearses the happy journey back to their homeland. Nature itself will be rejoicing in Israel's sure return.

21

On Mark 1:7–11
Context

Narratively, Mark's story of the baptism of Jesus comes after his account of the ministry of John the Baptist in the wilderness (1:1/2–8). In addition to Jesus' baptism, today's Gospel reading includes the Baptist's words about the superiority of the one coming after him who will baptize with the Holy Spirit (vv. 7–8). The selection from the *Revised Common Lectionary* reaches even further back to the appearance of John in the wilderness (v. 4). Verses 4–6 were discussed in chapter2: Second Sunday of Advent.

Questions

1. What are the scriptural texts the voice from heaven is quoting, and what significance do they have for understanding this scene?
2. What is the narrative and ideological function of the revelation "from heaven" (v. 11)?
3. In contrast with Matthew's parallel story, who is hearing the voice from heaven in Mark's account, and how does it change the story?

⊷ ❦ ❧ ⊶

4. Can you identify any part of the testimony of the Baptist (vv. 7–8) that remains unfulfilled, at the narrative level, in Mark's Gospel?
5. What do you think of the apocalyptic story-world presented in Mark 1:9–11, that is, what is the narrative function of the splitting of the heavens, the descent of the Spirit upon Jesus, and the voice from heaven?
6. What is in your view the function of this story?

Interpretive points

1. *John and Jesus.* John's statement about the superiority of Jesus (vv. 7–8) would have no validity and authority unless he himself has already been legitimated. Such legitimating is the purpose of the previous verses. Mark 1:2–6 has presented John as not only fulfilling the prophecy of Isaiah (vv. 2–3), but also dressing and eating like the prophet Elijah (2 Kgs 1:8). It will be remembered that Elijah was identified in Malachi 4:5 as the "messenger" who is sent to prepare the way before the Lord (Mal 3:1). Legitimated by Scriptural texts and the obvious reference to the re-

turn of Elijah, John, in turn, legitimates the one who is greater, coming after him and baptizing people with the Holy Spirit (vv. 7–8).

2. *Another legitimating scene.* The baptism story continues the legitimating process of Jesus with his apocalyptic vision of the heavens tearing, the descent of the Spirit like a dove upon him, and the voice from heaven acknowledging him as God's Son, the beloved (9–11). Our use of the word "legitimating," though it may sound alien to some, hopefully will draw attention to the rhetorical purpose of Mark's introduction to his Gospel. In addition to the information supplied by the narrator in the title (v. 1), readers can now rely on the divinely sent witness of John the Baptist and, still more importantly, on the voice from heaven, confirming what the title has already implied about Jesus. This being said, readers should be aware that this is a Christological reading of First Testament texts. It is the Christian faith and interpretation of such texts that ultimately provide the legitimating.

3. *Inside information, again.* Returning to something discussed earlier (Second Sunday of Advent), readers of this story are privy to information about Jesus that will not be available to the various characters of the Gospel narrative. Contrary to the parallel version of Matthew, the voice in Mark speaks only to Jesus, not to the crowd. This means that only Jesus and the readers know about his call or commissioning at the Jordan. Yet, despite such knowledge, readers still have a lot left to learn from the characters' misunderstandings and misconstructions of Jesus' identity and mission throughout the Gospel.

4. *Divine interpretation of Scripture!* Who would expect God to use the Scriptures to inform Jesus of his real identity and mission? This divine declaration combines two passages from Scripture: Psalm 2:7 (You are my son—God's word to the Davidic ruler) and Isaiah 42:1b (my servant . . . in whom my soul delights and whose mission is to achieve justice for the nations). Together, these two texts define Jesus' commissioning as God's beloved Son (see 1:1). The addition of the term "beloved"—if in any way reminiscent of God's reference to Abraham's only beloved son, Isaac (Gen 22:2, 12)—might be construed as a hint to Jesus' future fate.

5. *Jesus' commissioning.* The focus of Mark's account of Jesus' baptism (1:9–11) is not on the ritual, merely mentioned in verse 9, but on what Jesus is seeing and hearing after the baptism. It is through this vision that Jesus learns of his identity and mission. With the entire vision expressed in what is generally viewed as apocalyptic language, readers should pay more attention to its symbolic meaning than to its physical occurrence.

Pastoral and homiletical notes

1. *Following Mark's lead.* Taking its cue from the evangelist, the Church intends for Christians to first hear of Jesus' baptism before they listen, Sunday after Sunday, to the events of his ministry. Following Mark's lead, preachers should focus, therefore, not on the baptism of Jesus per se, but on what the vision conveys in terms of Jesus' identity and mission.

2. *History and symbol.* Harking back to our considerations on the legitimating character of Mark's introduction to his Gospel, preachers have a great opportunity to help their congregations better understand the literary genre of such stories as the baptism of Jesus. While his baptism at the hands of John the Baptist is deemed by all accounts to be a historical event, the vision that follows the ritual is of a different order and should be treated as such. This is easier done and said in Mark who, contrary to what appears in Matthew, refers only to the personal experience of Jesus.

3. *Changing the combination.* It is not clear why it was decided in 1998 to propose Isaiah 55:1–11 as an alternative reading to Isaiah 42:1–7 in the *Roman Catholic Lectionary*. Although Isaiah 55 is a meaningful text, its connection with the Gospel of the day is not immediately apparent. It may be that readers are invited to see in Jesus—acknowledged as God's son in the Gospel passage—the incarnation of the Lord's reliable and effective word (Isa 55:10–11). It may also be that this combination is meant to draw attention to the fact that God continues through Jesus to act in ways that are "higher than your ways" (v. 9). This Christian reading is perfectly valid and legitimate. It should not be understood, however, as minimizing, still less invalidating, the interpretations given in the historical context of the Jewish Scriptures.

LENTEN SEASON

The season of Lent is, like Advent, a time of preparation, a forty-day long preparation for the Easter Triduum, the greatest feast of the liturgical year. Because they celebrate during those three intensive days the central mystery of God's salvation in Christ, Christians are invited during Lent to prepare their mind and heart to this extraordinary action of God on behalf of humanity. Not primarily through penance, sacrifices, and repentance, as it has traditionally been understood, but through a communal reflection on, and understanding of, the choices and commitments that faith in a risen crucified Messiah (to stay within Mark's Gospel) will exact from Christians. Such an understanding is made easier by the first Sunday's Gospel text on the "temptations" or rather on the test of Jesus. Not surprisingly, calls and invitations to share with the needy among us, in our society, and even in the world at large, have replaced, in many Churches today, the traditionally more penitential aspect of Lent.

In the year of Mark, congregations will hear only two passages from that Gospel during the season of Lent: the temptations of Jesus (1:12–15) on the first Sunday, and on the second, the transfiguration (9:2–9). For the last three Sundays of Lent, the lectionary turns to passages from the Gospel of John (2:13–25; 3:14–21; and 12:20–33). Wherever a catechumenate program is on, these texts may be replaced by the readings of year A, also taken from John (John 4, 9, 11), which seems more appropriate to the thematic of baptism.

4. First Sunday of Lent

Year B

<table>
<tr><td>Roman Catholic L</td><td>Revised Common L</td></tr>
<tr><td>Genesis 9:8–15</td><td>Genesis 9:8–17</td></tr>
<tr><td>Mark 1:12–15</td><td>Mark 1:9–15</td></tr>
</table>

The Test of a Beloved Son
(Mark 1:9–15)

On Genesis 9:8–15

Although a clearly composite construction, the story of the flood, as it now stands, is a well-structured narrative. A return to the primitive chaos (7:17–24), caused by a grieving God's decision to destroy humanity and all living creatures (6:7), is turned around when God remembers Noah and all the living creatures (8:1a), to give way to the creation of a new world order of things (8:1b–5). This new world order is sealed by the divine promise that never again (repeated twice) will God curse the earth and destroy its living creatures because of a humanity inclined to evil from youth (8:21–22). Today's selection forms the second half of the conclusion to the flood narrative. It is in a different world, henceforth characterized by violence and sinfulness, that Noah and his family are blessed by God and urged to be fruitful and fill the earth (9:1–7). It is with this new and different world and all its inhabitants that God establishes a covenant and sets the rainbow as insurance for humanity (9:8–17). This is a universal covenant, made with all humanity and the whole earth, eternal and irreversible (vv. 8–11), of which the rainbow will be a constant reminder to God (vv. 12–17).

ON MARK 1:9–15
Context

The stories of Jesus' baptism in the Jordan (1:9–11) and his testing in the wilderness (vv. 12–13) make up the second and third subunit of what is generally viewed as the prologue or introduction to the Gospel of Mark. They follow Mark's account of the ministry of John the Baptist, the legitimately appointed forerunner of Jesus (see above comments on the Second Sunday of Advent). Whether this introduction should also include the summary or beginning of Jesus' proclamation in Galilee (vv. 14–15) is, as we mentioned earlier (see Second Sunday of Advent), still much disputed.

Since the story of Jesus' baptism was treated earlier for the feast of the same name, our attention will focus—in accordance of the *Roman Catholic Lectionary* selection—on the account of the temptation of Jesus and the programmatic summary of his teaching in Galilee (1:12–15).

Questions

1. To which biblical tradition belongs Jesus' forty days of "testing" or temptation in the wilderness?
2. Why do you think Mark informs the reader, so early in his narrative, of Jesus' encounter with Satan and what are we told of the outcome of this encounter?
3. What is your interpretation of Mark's (unique) reference to Jesus' presence with the wild beasts? Can you think of any connection to the next unit (1:14–15)?

⊢— ❧ ❧ —⊣

4. Why do you think Jesus needs to be "driven out" (actually, thrown out) into the wilderness by the Spirit, even though he is already in the wilderness (1:3–4)?
5. How significant is the notice that Jesus' return to Galilee to begin his ministry follows shortly after the arrest and imprisonment of John?
6. In your view, how should the expression "proclaiming the good news of God" be read, as good news about God or from God?
7. How do you image the "kingdom" of God and in this context what meaning has the directive to "repent"?

Interpretive points

1. *Conflict on the horizon.* Contrary to Matthew and Luke's accounts of the temptations of Jesus, Mark says nothing about the nature of the test he faces in the wilderness. Although an echo of the experience of Israel's 40 years of test in the wilderness cannot be excluded altogether, it is certainly not the primary focus of this rather short account. Clearly, Mark's interest lies with introducing the central conflict between Jesus, God's Son, and the forces of evil, represented here by Satan, which will unfold in the rest of the Gospel narrative. While the outcome of their encounter is not entirely clear, Jesus' many subsequent expulsions of demons (starting almost immediately in 1:21–28) and his assertion that no one can do what he is doing without first binding the strong man, Satan (3:27), will certainly remind readers of that initial experience in the wilderness.

2. *What of the wild beasts?* Of the three evangelists reporting on this episode, Mark is the only one to mention the presence of the wild beasts. What their company represents, however, is not at all evident. Are they symbolizing the forces of evil or should they be viewed as referring to the Isaian vision of peace, or even as a restoration of the paradisiacal harmony between human beings and (wild) animals? Interesting though they are, the last two suggestions do not fully explain the presence of angels ministering to Jesus during the whole experience.

3. *Jesus' embodiment of God's Rule.* Whether it concludes the prologue to the Gospel or is the beginning of Jesus' entry into the public arena, Mark 1:14–15 is a paradigmatic statement of Jesus' entire ministry. His proclamation of the good news of God will incorporate all his subsequent activities of healing, exorcising, and teaching. As the very location of the two Greek verbs indicate (fulfilled is the time, at hand is the sovereign rule of God), the emphasis is not on the designated time *(kairos)*, but its fulfillment, not on God's sovereign rule, but on the fact that this rule is already being experienced (the best translation) with Jesus' coming. Such a view has the merit of highlighting the ethical nature of the next teaching.

4. *Precondition or response?* Jesus' last words, "Repent and believe in the good news" have been understood in two different ways, whether read in se-

quential order or taken as the flip sides of the same coin. In the first instance, the *metanoia*, understood primarily in terms of regret or repentance, is seen as a precondition for experiencing the sovereign rule of God. Conversely, the second reading—equating repent with believe in (on the basis of) the good news—preserves the primary meaning of *metanoia* as a complete turning back or reversal of mindset, and sees it as a response to the good news of God's salvation in Jesus Christ. Although less traditional, this second reading appears more in line with the whole Gospel presentation.

Pastoral and homiletical notes

1. *Converting to the Good News.* The addition of the programmatic statement of Jesus' ministry to Mark's brief account of Jesus' temptation in the wilderness may be a great occasion for preachers to help their congregations focus on the kind of *metanoia* (response?) needed to prepare for celebrating the greatest Christian paradox of Holy Week.

2. *No easy "conversion."* As the rest of the Gospel will show, Jesus' proclamation of the Good News of God (and of God's sovereign rule) will demand a turning back of 180 degrees, a reversal of mindset, priorities, and perspectives. At this point, preachers should remember that, in Mark's Gospel, the disciples, the male disciples in particular, never achieve this radical "conversion" to Jesus' message.

3. *Life is an ongoing test.* In historicizing the temptations of Jesus at the beginning of Jesus' ministry, Mark, like Matthew and Luke, is telling us that his mission (see 1:14–15) will not be an easy one. No preaching on the story of Jesus' temptations should overlook the struggles, trials, or tests that he is about to face during his ministry, down to his very death.

4. *God's enduring covenant.* One way to connect the first reading to the Gospel text of today is to see in the eternal covenant with Noah and his family (Gen 9:8–17) the work of a loving God who cares for the earth and humanity, despite their inclination to evil from youth. It is the work of this same loving and caring God that Jesus urges the people of Galilee—and us—to continue to embrace and experience.

5. SECOND SUNDAY OF LENT
Year B

Roman Catholic L
Genesis 22:1–2, 9–13, 15–18
Mark 9:2–10

Revised Common L
Genesis 17:1–7, 15–16
Mark 8:31–38

THIS IS MY SON, MY BELOVED, LISTEN TO HIM!
(MARK 9:2–10)

ON GENESIS 22:1–2, 9–13, 15–18

Today's first reading, generally referred to as the binding or sacrifice of Isaac, could be more appropriately referred to as God's test of Abraham's faith. In fact, in the entire saga of Abraham, this is the last and greatest trial or test that Israel's ancestor has to face. Here, in stark contrast with his previous experiences, Abraham amazingly trusts in, and is obedient to, God's command. Ostensibly relieved that Abraham has passed the test, the Lord can hardly wait to reaffirm the promises made to him when called to leave country and family for an unknown land (22:17–18; cf. 12:1–3).

Perhaps at a more historically-oriented level, the remarkable saga of Abraham, this story included, speaks loud and clear to Israel's frequent experiences of God's promises being withdrawn and restored. Throughout this saga, one is frequently left to wonder who, in fact, is being tested—Abraham/Israel or God. One of the merits of this reading is that it eases some of the disturbing questions raised by the text, not least of which is what kind of a God would require such a sacrifice. It is doubtful, however, that this passage in the *Roman Catholic Lectionary* was chosen because of either of these readings. It more likely reflects the focus of the Christian tradition on seeing in Isaac a type of the crucified Christ.

ON MARK 9:2–10

Context

(For the study guide on Mark 8:31–38, the *Revised Common Lectionary* reading, see chapter 25.)

Cast in the form of a long journey "on the way" to Jerusalem, the fourth major section of the Gospel of Mark (8:27—10:52) is structured around Jesus' three predictions of his passion, death, and resurrection (8:31; 9:31; 10:33–34). Each prediction is followed by misunderstandings from the disciples, which, in turn, cause Jesus to impart some new teachings concerning discipleship. On this first occasion, Peter's opposition to Jesus' prediction is immediately followed by a rebuke from Jesus (vv. 31–33) and short instructions on the *cost* of discipleship (vv. 34–38). Next follows the story of the Transfiguration (9:2–9), which is preceded by a rather enigmatic claim by Jesus that "there are some standing here who will not taste death until they see that the *basileia* of God has come with power" (9:1).

Most Bibles and many commentaries separate the story of the Transfiguration proper (vv. 2–8) from verses 9–13. While the connection between verses 10 and 11–13 is not evident, it is more difficult to exclude verse 9 from the Transfiguration story. Its obvious connection with verse 2 and, for that matter, with verse 10 makes its exclusion incomprehensible. Notwithstanding the choice made by the lectionaries, readers should take stock of the fact that the Transfiguration story is bracketed by Jesus' discourse on suffering (8:31–38 and 9:12–13, 30–31). Indeed, this context may hold the key to its rhetorical function in the narrative.

Questions

1. Identify three major differences between Mark's distinctive narrative and Luke's version of this same story (9:28–37). (A Gospel Synopsis or Parallels would be most helpful to carry this exercise.)
2. What narrative function do Elijah and Moses serve in this story?
3. Where has this heavenly voice first been heard in Mark and to whom was it addressed? What do you think is the narrative and rhetorical function of verse 7 in this story for the disciples and readers respectively?

⊹ ❦ ❧ ⊹

4. How has Mark prepared readers for Peter's apparent failure to understand what is going on (v. 5)?

5. In what sense, if any, can this episode be considered a "legitimating" scene for Jesus, the disciples, and the readers?

6. Which of these scholarly explanations would best fit your own reading of the story: A misplaced resurrection narrative; a symbolic interpretation of the disciples' experience of Jesus; an apocalyptic vision; a dramatized historical account; or, finally, a christophany or appearance of Christ?

Interpretive points

1. *What kind of story is this?* If only because of their graphic reference to the "divine" or supernatural world, both the stories of the Transfiguration and baptism of Jesus will raise questions about their "literary genre." Such elements as the transformation of Jesus, the appearance of Elijah and Moses, the biblical cloud, and the heavenly voice, as well as echoes from the book of Exodus (Exod 24 and 34), make all the more complex the task of identifying the "genre." Question 7 introduces various scholarly solutions to this problem and calls for your own thoughts on this important interpretive issue.

2. *What happened at the Transfiguration?* Whatever answer is given to the question of genre, it does not preclude from asking the historical question of what, if anything, happened "on the mountain." For a recent attempt at digging up the historical core of this "episode" in the life of Jesus, see the methodologically interesting article of Jerome Murphy-O'Connor: "What Really Happened at the Transfiguration?" (In *Bible Review*, Fall 1987). Such a search should not undermine, however, still less replace, the quest for the rhetorical function of the narrative in Mark.

3. *Whose experience?* Luke's version of the Transfiguration refers to a change in Jesus' face. It clearly speaks primarily to a personal experience of Jesus. This is less clear in the NRSV due to a mistranslation in verse 30. Contrary to Luke's version, Mark has the three disciples experience the "metamorphosis" or transformation of Jesus. Taking

the context or location of the story into account, in particular Jesus' words on suffering and the cost of discipleship, it is surprising how little impact this experience seems to have upon the disciples' understanding of Jesus. Not only is Peter completely irrational (9:6), but also he and his companions will soon be wondering, on the way down the mountain, about "what this rising from the dead could mean" (9:10). Furthermore, as the rest of this section unfolds, things do not appear to become any clearer to the disciples.

4. *A challenge to readers.* This story makes more sense if understood as being directed to the readers. They know Jesus' true identity from the very beginning of Mark's narrative. Unlike the disciples in the story, they have learned from the onset that Jesus is "Christ [and] Son of God" (1:1). At his baptism by John, they have heard the heavenly voice acknowledge Jesus as "my Son, the Beloved, [in whom] I am well pleased" (1:11). It is this same heavenly voice that they now hear urging them to "listen to" what [my beloved Son] Jesus has to say. In light of the context, the real function of the story may be to educate readers in this new teaching of Jesus "on the way to Jerusalem."

5. *Beware of anti-Judaism, again!* Although the "heavenly" command to listen to Jesus cannot be taken lightly, it should not become an occasion to undermine or even invalidate the teachings of Elijah (the prophets) and Moses (Torah), the conversation partners of Jesus in the story.

Pastoral and homiletical notes

1. *Not forgetting the context.* The *Revised Common Lectionary* suggests Mark 8:31–38 as an alternative reading for this second Sunday of Lent. These verses make up, as noted earlier, part of the immediate context to the mountain experience. Whether they are read or not on this day, these verses should not be ignored.

2. *In touch with the transcendant.* Preaching on the Transfiguration story will inevitably involve addressing the crucial issue of how the transcendant is revealed within our world today. Unless Christians can be

shown that the event keeps happening, not on the mountain top, but again and again in their every day lives, the risk is great for such a story to become irrelevant.

3. *Whose test?* The story of Abraham's testing by God appears to fit better the alternative Gospel reading, suggested in the *Revised Common Lectionary*. Because of the Lenten context in which the reading is located, Roman Catholic preachers may be tempted to move away from the Gospel story and focus their reflection on the "testing" of Abraham and the "sacrifice" demanded of him. If pursued, this line of thought may lead to a salutary reflection on the kind of God who is ready to "sacrifice" his own Son, and to ask other people to do the same.

Holy Week and the Easter Season

Holy Week, particularly the Easter Triduum, is more than the liturgical celebration or reminiscence of the last moments of Jesus' life on earth and of the first news of his resurrection heard on Easter vigil. This week is an essential part of the Easter celebration, which will end, liturgically, some 40 and 50 days later with the feasts of Ascension and Pentecost. Though liturgically separated in time, Jesus' death, resurrection, and ascension, as well as the outpouring of the Spirit on Pentecost, are aspects of the one and same mystery of God's salvation in Christ. The narrative presentation of Christ' redemptive work as separate and consecutive events may come from Luke-Acts, but its unified presentation owes to John's well-known construal of Jesus' glorification on the cross. It is, therefore, no accident to have the *Roman Catholic Lectionary* recommend readings from the Fourth Gospel for most of that week, Monday to Good Friday.

In all three years of the lectionary cycle, texts from the respective Gospels will be used at both the beginning and the end of Holy Week. In the year of Mark, his versions of the Entry into Jerusalem (11:1–11) and of the passion (14–15) are read on Palm Sunday, while at the Easter vigil Christians will hear his story of the empty tomb (16:1–8)—the only text from Mark's Gospel to be heard during the Easter season.

As important as Holy Week is to Christians, Jews still dread this time, Good Friday in particular, which has not been good to them. They cannot easily forget the humiliations inflicted upon them by Christians on the very day they remembered the death of their Lord Jesus. Now that the charge of deicide brought against Jews of all times has been condemned and rejected by all mainline Churches, preachers and liturgists will do their best during that week, especially on Good Friday, to eliminate from texts, rituals, hymns, and prayers, anything that could be disparaging to our Jewish sisters and brothers.

6A. PALM LITURGY
Year B

Roman Catholic L   *Revised Common L*
Mark 11:1–10   Mark 11:1–11

JESUS' APPROACH TO JERUSALEM
(MARK 11:1–10)

ON MARK 11:1–10
Context

Mark 11:1–11 opens a new section, which describes Jesus' final week in and around Jerusalem. For the first and only time in Mark, Jesus and his disciples arrive near the city and a new stage in the narrative begins. This final stage can be divided into two major sections: the controversy of Jesus with Jerusalem and its institutions (11–13) and the passion narrative (14–15).

Since Mark 8:26, Jesus has been slowly moving towards Jerusalem, followed by his disciples. Along the way, he instructed them about his upcoming fate in Jerusalem and its significance for his followers. The healing of blind Bartimaeus and his decision to follow Jesus "on the way" (10:46–52) is both a good ending to the previous section and a signal that it is time to move from Jericho to the city of Jerusalem. As the journey nears its end, so too does Jesus' private teaching to his disciples—immediately replaced by public confrontation in and around the city. This confrontation, initiated by Jesus, pushes the authorities to question by which authority Jesus does what he does. Then, as we move into the passion narrative, this initiative is now to be taken by the authorities, reaching its climax in Jesus' crucifixion in chapter 15.

Questions

1. Why do you think is so much attention given to the preparation of the event (vv. 1b–7)?
2. Who are the chief participants in this event: the crowds and the disciples following Jesus or/and the people from the city? Support your answer.
3. How do you interpret the acclamation in verses 9–10 and why do you think Jesus is connected with David?

✢ ✢ ✢

4. Which prophetic text from the First Testament might "explain" the actions of Jesus as he approaches the city?
5. Is there anything in the text that warrants the usual designation of this episode as "The triumphal entry into Jerusalem"?
6. How does a comparison of Mark's story with Matthew's version (21:1–11) help to focus on what the Markan text says and does not say?

Interpretive points

1. *A messianic entrance?* All commentators of Mark 11:1–11 understand this episode in messianic terms, on account of the echo of Zechariah's prophecy (Zech 9:9) and the "nationalistic" shouts of the crowd about the coming of the kingdom of David (Mark 11:10). Although Mark, unlike Matthew and John, does not quote the passage from Zechariah, there is general agreement that the depiction of Jesus approaching the city on a donkey (of all animals!) should send readers back to the vision of the prophet.

2. *Jesus' symbolic rejection of a nationalistic kingdom.* There is also general agreement on the *nationalistic* interpretation of the event by the disciples and the crowd (in the text). In this, they are no different from the majority of interpreters and readers who have generally understood, and continue to understand this story as the triumphal entry into Jerusalem of its Messiah. Yet, not all scholars accept this traditional reading of this story, at least with regard to Jesus. While clearly pointing to the text of Zechariah, Jesus' well organized "choreographed action"

also embodies the prophet's rather peculiar description of the messiah-king's triumphant and victorious coming, "humble and riding on a donkey, on a colt, the foal of a donkey" (Zech 9:9). Such a description seems to contrast with the apparently nationalistic acclamation of the crowd and disciples. It would not be the first time in Mark that the disciples are totally obtuse to Jesus' identity.

3. *No triumphal "entry" into Jerusalem!* Although the story is still generally understood as the triumphal entry into Jerusalem, including, I would suggest in the palm liturgy, the "procession"—with its display of nationalistic fervor—occurs, not in the city, but on the way to the city: "When they were *approaching* Jerusalem . . ." (11:1). There is nothing in verse 11 to suggest a triumphant "entrance" into Jerusalem (compare with Matt 21:10–11 where the "celebration" appears to continue right into the city). After the "messianic" celebration is over, Jesus enters the city by himself and, unobserved, goes into the Temple and, after taking a good look around (to reconnoiter and see what needs to be done the next day? e.g. 11:15–19), returns to Bethany, accompanied by the Twelve.

4. *Two different "crowds"!* The lack of any involvement from the people of Jerusalem in the "messianic" celebration, occurring on the outskirts of the city, allows us to solve a problem that has long puzzled interpreters. How can such an enthusiastic crowd so quickly change their coats and request Jesus' crucifixion from Pilate (15:12–13)? In Mark, they are not the same crowds! Nothing in the text of Mark allows us to identify the disciples and the large crowd that followed Jesus since he left Jericho (10:46) with the crowd from Jerusalem who, later on, will urge Pilate to release Barabbas and crucify Jesus (15:11–13).

Pastoral and homiletical notes

1. *Reinterpreting the "triumphal entry."* Mark's story of Jesus' approach to Jerusalem is read on Palm Sunday as part of the palm liturgy. Its juxtaposition with the passion narrative constitutes a most interesting hermeneutical decision. Whatever interpretation is given of the palm episode, its true message should not be concealed. Unlike the disci-

ples and the large crowd in the story, Christians, as readers, are informed of the kind of (suffering) Messiah that Jesus is. Talk of a "triumphal entry" into Jerusalem may not only be misreading the Gospel text, but also compromising its very purpose.

2. *Embracing a suffering Messiah.* At the beginning of Holy Week, this new example of misunderstanding of Jesus' messianic status by both disciples and the crowd provide preachers with a golden opportunity to reflect on the difficulty for all to embrace and commit to a suffering Messiah. Mark's portrayal of the unperceptive (male) disciples reaches its climax during the passion with their total collapse. Judas will betray Jesus, Peter will deny him, and in the end, they will all desert him (15:50). Admittedly, this is not the end of their story. At the last meal with his disciples, Jesus predicts their desertion, only to follow up almost in the same breath promising their reconciliation in Galilee (14:27–28). It may, however, be better to leave this extraordinary promise for the Easter Vigil when Christians will again hear these very same words on the lips of a "young man, dressed in a white robe, sitting on the right side (of the tomb)" (16:5).

3. *Preaching on the palm episode!* There are sound liturgical reasons for questioning the purpose of having the passion narrative read at all on Palm Sunday. One of these reasons is that this reading anticipates events (passion and crucifixion of Jesus) that liturgically will be celebrated later in the week. I would like to suggest that there are also, as the above pastoral notes have indicated, good liturgical (and theological) reasons for preachers on this Sunday to focus entirely on the meaning of the palm episode.

6B. PALM SUNDAY OF THE LORD'S PASSION
Year B

Roman Catholic L   *Revised Common L*

Isaiah 50:4–7   Isaiah 50:4–9a

Mark 14:1—15:47   Mark 14:1—15:47

THE PASSION NARRATIVE
(MARK 14—15)

ON ISAIAH 50:4–7

For the study guide on Isaiah 50:4–7, see chapter 25.

ON MARK 14—15
Context

Interrupted by the Little Apocalypse of chapter 13, the Markan story line of Jesus resumes in 14:1 with the mention that "the chief priests and the scribes were looking for a way to arrest Jesus by stealth and kill him." Readers already have met this coalition of forces against Jesus in the controversy section of Mark 11—12. Following upon Jesus' purifying action in the Temple, they have been "looking for a way to kill him" (11:18). Some time later, now joined by the elders, they are back at work, questioning what authority Jesus has to do these things (11:27), but failing to arrest him for fear of the crowds (12:12). Jesus' prophetic words concerning his coming death in Jerusalem (8:31 and 10:33; cf. also 9:31), uttered in the presence of his disciples, are now about to be implemented in the passion narrative.

Questions

1. Why do you think Mark would frame the passion narrative with two stories involving women as prominent characters (14:3–9 and 15:40–41, 47)?
2. What could be a possible narrative or theological reason behind Mark's bracketing of the trial of Jesus before the High Priest by the accounts of Peter's denials (14:54–72)?
3. What narrative/theological function do the following narrative events serve?
   - Darkness at noon (15:33)
   - Tearing of the curtain in the Temple (15:38)
   - Confession of the Roman centurion (15:39)

4. What do you think, at this point of the narrative, brings Jesus to acknowledge that he is the Christ/Messiah, the Son of the Blessed One (14:60–62)?
5. What, in your view, underlies the frequent use of psalms and prophetic utterances in the passion narrative?
6. Considering that the Jewish authorities are in part made responsible for the death of Jesus in Mark's passion narrative, what could now be done to eliminate any anti-Jewish connotations from such texts?
7. What do you think of Jesus' "hard words" to the betrayer in 14:21 and how does it compare with his reaction to Peter's denials?

Interpretive points

1. *Reading the passion with Jesus.* Mark's passion narrative can be read in different ways, two of which are particularly significant. It can be read through the eyes of its main character, Jesus, or through the eyes of the disciples, his followers. The Markan story of the passion has often been described as a "Way of the Cross." This designation implies that Mark, perhaps more than the other three evangelists, accentuates the sufferings of Jesus on his way to the cross. Mark's account, to be sure, is filled not only with pain and torture. There are a few moments where the "divine" Jesus shines through, but in the end, the reader is left with images of a very human Jesus. He strug-

gles in Gethsemane and on the cross, is mocked and ridiculed by both Jewish and Roman mobs, and most significant of all, abandoned by almost everyone: Judas, Peter, the disciples, the crowd, Pilate, and finally God. In Mark, Jesus dies alone, except for his women followers watching from a distance.

This Markan presentation of Jesus should not be isolated from the context of his life. Without the story of his public ministry, interspersed, as we have seen, with numerous attempts made on his life, the death of Jesus loses its meaning. By making a spectacle of Jesus' passion and death, totally disconnected from his life, flashbacks notwithstanding, Mel Gibson's presentation of the *Passion of the Christ* trivializes the actual suffering of Jesus as well as his call and mission. In Mark's terms, Jesus' passion and death was the price he had to pay for remaining faithful to this call and mission. Jesus' understanding of his mission in terms of "service" (10:45) is what led him to the cross, not the other way round.

2. *Reading the passion with the Twelve.* One other interesting way of reading this passion narrative is through the eyes of the male disciples. By now, the reader should be well acquainted with Mark's profile of their obtuseness. How are they going to fare in the passion? Things do not start very well for the Twelve. First, readers are quickly informed of Judas' plan to betray Jesus to the chief priests (14:10–11). The betrayal is confirmed soon afterwards when Jesus, at table with the Twelve, issues one of his harshest words of judgment on his betrayer (14:17–21). Second, the entire group of disciples will not fare much better since, according to Jesus, they will all soon be scandalized or fall away. Peter himself, despite bragging about his courage, is told that he will deny Jesus three times that very night (14:26–31).

The next scene, in a place called Gethsemane, is remarkable in many respects, and full of lessons for both disciples and readers. Jesus' own struggle and ultimate trust in God form the backdrop for the disciples' failure to "watch and pray." The disciples still have to learn about the power of prayer. Not surprisingly, they are all soon shown to desert Jesus (14:50). In contrast to Jesus' resolution, boldness, and courage before the High Priest, Peter, weak and fearful, quickly fails to acknowledge any connection to his beloved Master (14:66–72).

3. *Presence of women at the cross.* Other "disciples" are present in the passion narrative that, some would say, constitutes a welcome contrast to the Twelve. Two stories where women figure prominently, "frame" the entire passion narrative. The narrative opens with the story of an unknown woman who anoints Jesus as the suffering messiah/king and who, for this action, is acknowledged by Jesus with words that have, unfortunately, been ignored for far too long (14:9). The passion narrative closes with Jesus abandoned on the cross, except for his women disciples who watch from a distance. These women, we are told, had "followed" Jesus in Galilee and had come with him all the way to Jerusalem (15:40, 47)!

4. *A Gentile's remarkable confession.* It cannot be an accident that the most remarkable human confession made of Jesus in Mark comes from a Gentile, immediately following his death (15:39). This confession harks back, not only to Jesus' own claim before the high priest, earlier on in the passion (14:62), but also to the opening verse of Mark's Gospel (1:1).

Pastoral and homiletical notes

1. *Preaching on the passion.* For Gerard Sloyan, it makes little sense to read the whole passion story on Palm Sunday before the events it contains are *liturgically* celebrated during Holy Week. It would be more profitable and more liturgically sound on this Sunday to proclaim the death and resurrection of Jesus, as Mark does no less than three times in his Gospel (8:31; 9:31; 10:33). Always according to Sloyan, Mark 14:26–51 followed by 16:1–8 would be a more suitable Gospel passage for this Sunday.

    Whatever decision is made, preachers on this day should use the passion narrative or portions of it as interpretive keys for understanding the so-called triumphal entry of Jesus into Jerusalem. Liturgically, in many Churches, the "triumphal entry" precedes the liturgy of the Word. These interpretive keys may better represent Mark's presentation of Jesus' approach to Jerusalem and what it will really entail.

2. *Using the Scriptures.* Mark uses many passages from the psalms and the prophets to theologically legitimate, not only the death of Jesus, but also

the various events that make up the entire passion narrative. These citations provide a key to preachers for interpreting this important text.

3. *An opportunity to address anti-Judaism!* The anti-Jewish potential of the passion narratives is a live issue for Churches at all times, but especially so during Holy Week. Perhaps more than any other texts, these narratives have contributed to the development of the "deicide charge" leveled against the entire Jewish people. Following the decision by all mainline Christian Churches to reject 2000 years of this teaching of contempt, preachers at this particular time should welcome the opportunity to address any remnant of Christian anti-Judaism or anti-Semitism.

4. *About dramatizations.* Given a tendency to dramatize the passion narratives in many congregations, preachers will find a useful tool in the *Criteria for the Evaluation of Dramatizations of the Passion*, published by the U.S. Bishops' Committee on Ecumenical and Interreligious Affairs. A simple disclaimer like the following, inspired from Vatican II's declaration *Nostra Aetate*, might make all the difference:

> Christians, hearing the Passion Narratives, should recall that although the Gospel narratives suggest that some Jewish authorities and those who follow their lead press for the death of Jesus, neither all Jews indiscriminately at that time, nor Jews today, could be charged with his execution.

5. *Away with supersessionism.* Although legitimate, the paring of Isaiah 50:4–7(9) with the passion narrative could foster a supersessionist reading of the first passage that, today, must be rejected. In accordance with an important insight from the latest document issued by the Pontifical Biblical Commission *(The Jewish People and their Sacred Scriptures in the Christian Bible)*, preachers should now make sure that a perfectly valid Christian or Christological reading of a First Testament passage is not perceived as invalidating the reading that Jews make of the same passage.

7. EASTER VIGIL
Year B

Roman Catholic L	***Revised Common L***
7 First Testament readings	7 First Testament readings
Mark 16:1–8	Mark 16:1–8

HEARING THE EASTER MESSAGE
(MARK 16:1–8)

ON THE FIRST TESTAMENT READINGS

It has been the practice of Churches at the Easter Vigil to read a collection of passages from the First Testament, seven in all. This collection covers a wide range of readings, the purpose of which is to summon up the major events of what has been called the History of Salvation. Although preachers are not expected to preach on any one of these readings, these can hardly be ignored in light of the Second Testament readings that follow. Both of these readings speak, each in their own way, to the fulfillment of God's plan of salvation in Christ.

ON MARK 16:1–8
Context

The story of the visit to the tomb by three women at sunrise on the first day of the week follows, quite naturally, on the narrative of Jesus' burial on the eve of Sabbath. This burial story ends with the strange comment that two of these women, Mary Magdalene and Mary the mother of Jesus, have seen where the body was laid (15:47). These three women disciples, along with others, are said to have followed Jesus to Jerusalem and watched his crucifixion "from a distance" (15:40). Although, in most Bibles, the Markan narrative is continued after Mark

16:8a, today's selection (16:1–8a) is generally viewed as the original conclusion to Mark's Gospel.

Questions

1. Can you think of any reason why so much attention is given at the beginning of the story to the outbreak of daylight (16:1–2)?
2. What do you think are the most important verses of this story and why?
3. How do you understand Mark 16:8 and what is different in Matthew's "rereading" of this verse (28:8)?

4. What is the difference between the prophetic action of the unknown woman in 14:3–9, and the anointing of Jesus' body after death by the women?
5. Some commentators relate the "young man dressed in a white robe" (v. 5) to the young man (same Greek word) who ran away naked, leaving his linen cloth, and deserting Jesus during the passion (14:51–52). What is the narrative function of these characters and how could they be related?
6. What does verse 7 add to one's understanding of discipleship in Mark, and why would Peter be singled out?
7. What narrative function does this story serve in the larger Gospel story of Mark?

Interpretive points

1. *Where does Mark end?* On account of the oldest Greek manuscript evidence and some important early theologians, Mark's rather strange ending (16:8a) is generally accepted, today, as the original conclusion to the Markan narrative. This, however, is a fairly recent view. Very early on, longer and more appropriate endings (referred to as the shorter and longer versions in our Bibles) were added, most likely, to transform, as did the other three evangelists, what appears to be a story ending in failure into one that ends successfully.

2. *What's up with the women?* The women's negative response to the angel's command that they should inform the disciples and Peter of

Jesus' desire to see all of them back in Galilee (vv. 7–8a) has baffled scholars since the earliest times, and continues to do so today. If Mark 16:8, as most interpreters now agree, is the original conclusion of the Gospel narrative, how should this strange, abrupt, and unhappy ending be interpreted? How should one understand the flight of the frightened women and their enigmatic silence (see Matt 28:8)? Should it be seen as a sign of human limitations in the presence of the divine or, just like their male counterparts, as a sign of their fallibility as disciples, or still, as a sign of one's inherent inability to come to terms with Jesus' resurrection? Whatever reading is accepted, it should not detract the reader from taking over the challenge faced by the women of the story, in response to the words of the young man concerning the Risen Jesus (v. 6).

3. *Words of grace and hope.* The absence of appearance stories in Mark's Gospel cannot be attributed to the author's ignorance of the resurrection. References to the resurrection abound in this Gospel, not the least of which are Jesus' three predictions of what is about to happen in Jerusalem (8:31; 9:31; and 10:34), and Jesus' promise to his disciples at the last supper that, once raised up, he would precede them into Galilee (14:28). Without appearance stories of the Risen Jesus, the reader of Mark 16 can only rely on the words of the messenger (vv. 6–7). Harking back to Jesus' promise at the last meal, these are words of hope and grace. They mean that the disciples' desertion of Jesus during the passion, Peter's denials of him, and perhaps even the women's possible failing, have been forgiven. Jesus, the crucified one, is going ahead of all of them to Galilee, where they will see him once again. As it has aptly been said, this is the Good News of Mark's Gospel.

4. *A new beginning.* Whatever one makes of verse 8, the last word belongs to the flesh and blood reader. Narratively, the ending makes sense only if it actually compels the reader to move beyond the narrative into an unknown future, grounded in Jesus' promise that they will see him once again in Galilee. The characters in the story must be allowed to give way to the readers outside the story. The outsiders, the readers, are the ones that will carry on the story, making it suc-

cessful with their return in faith to "Galilee." In other words, if they go back and start reading the Gospel again, and again and again, from its very beginning, they will continually meet the Risen Jesus! Mark had told readers right at the outset (1:1) that his story was only the *beginning* of the Good News of Jesus, Christ and Son of God. The conclusion of Mark's Gospel (16:1–8), including the puzzling verse 8, marks the end of the story, leaving to readers the task of once again meeting Jesus in Galilee where a new beginning awaits.

Pastoral and homiletical notes

1. *Beware of perceptions!* In Roman Catholic Churches, the Easter Vigil liturgy of the word moves rather slowly through a host of First Testament readings toward the light brought up by Christ, first symbolized in the fire ritual, then announced in the *Exultet*, and finally proclaimed in the Gospel reading. In most of these Churches, all First Testament readings will regrettably be read in darkness with the candles usually put out. No matter its positive rationale within Christianity (fulfillment, etc.), this ritual, unless checked, only reinforces the Christian perception that the "New" Testament Gospel has supplanted the "Old" Testament. Given the history of Christian anti-Semitism and the Churches' recent commitment to remove any trace of "substitution theology" (or supersessionism) from their teaching and practice, the time may have come to reevaluate some of our rituals. At the very least, congregations should be informed that the Christian understanding of these readings as preparation for the coming of Christ does, in no way, invalidate the way Jewish people understand or read their sacred texts today.

2. *The empty tomb: A means, not a proof!* Without the interpretive word of the "young man dressed in a white robe" (v. 6), the empty tomb would be nothing more than an empty tomb! As the parallel stories in Luke and John clearly show, faced with an empty tomb, the disciples take the women's report for idle talk, while Mary Magdalene thinks of a stolen body rather than of a resurrection. The purpose of this story is not to prove but rather to proclaim the resurrection of Jesus.

3. *Not to be taken for granted.* Some Roman Catholic congregations might not hear the famous verse 8 of Mark 16, which is not always included in the Gospel reading. It would be unfortunate if such an omission led preachers and Christians, to ignore or dismiss the difficulty, even for the original disciples, to believe in the resurrection of Jesus, bodily or otherwise. All three other Gospels, which present some appearances stories, are unanimous in mentioning amazement, questions, doubts, and even denials among Jesus' followers. Here in Mark, it is left to readers to hear the word of the "messenger" and, this time with the women among us, go back to Galilee where we will meet and hear Jesus. On the night of the Easter Vigil, I myself believe that congregations should hear and ponder the same challenges faced by the disciples, no more no less.

8. ASCENSION OF THE LORD
Year B

Roman Catholic L
Acts 1:1–11
Mark 16:15–20

Revised Common L
Acts 1:1–11
Luke 24:44–53

TAKEN UP INTO HEAVEN . . .
(MARK 16:15–20)

ON ACTS 1:1–11

Luke is the sole evangelist who provides a narrative of the Ascension of the Lord Jesus. He records this event twice, once at the end of his Gospel (24:50–53) and a second time at the beginning of his second volume, the book of Acts (1:2, 6–11). Surprisingly, these two accounts are at variance on the time of this event. It occurs on Easter Sunday in the Gospel (Luke 24:50–51) and, in the book of Acts (1:3), at the end of a forty-day period of appearances by the Risen Lord. Such a discrepancy would seem to confirm our earlier suggestion that Jesus' resurrection, ascension, and the outpouring of the Spirit are to be understood as a single event. In Acts, Luke has chosen to historicize this event, spreading it out in a time sequence presumably to emphasize the different aspects of the unique paschal mystery.

Today's first reading (Acts 1:1–11) can be divided into two parts, verses 1–5 and 6–11/12. In the first part, the author harks back to the narrative content of his first volume, from the beginning of Jesus' ministry all the way to his being taken up to heaven (vv. 1–2). Zeroing in on the appearances for which a different timeline is provided (v. 3), he then repeats Jesus' firm command to the apostles to wait in Jerusalem for their baptism with the Holy Spirit (vv. 4–5). The second part comprises three elements. First, Jesus dismisses his apostles' speculation concerning the time for the restoration of Israel (vv. 6–7). He then assures them of the Spirit's em-

53

powerment for their missionary task to be his witnesses from Jerusalem to the ends of the earth. The last verses (9–11/12) describe the ascension of Jesus into heaven, using echoes of prophet Elijah's own ascension into heaven and the translation of his spirit upon Elishah (2 Kings 2:9–11). As earlier on at the tomb, two heavenly messengers appear to correctly interpret this event for the disciples.

ON MARK 16:15–20
Context

Although Mark 16:9–20 is the traditional or canonical ending of Mark's Gospel narrative, its Markan authenticity is now almost universally questioned. For this reason, this section is clearly separated from the original Markan text in most Bibles. Not unlike the shorter ending, this longer ending is believed to be a second-century attempt to offset the strange reaction of the women to the messenger's command (16:8) as well as the absence of any appearance stories. Apart from a couple of signs that will validate the ministry of those who believe (harmless snake-handling and resistance to poison), this entire passage comes from a mix of traditions found in the other three Gospels, Matthew, Luke, and John: three successive appearances of Jesus, first to Mary Magdalene (vv. 9–11), then to two disciples (vv. 12–13), and finally to the Eleven themselves whom he reprimands for not believing the testimony of those who had seen him first (v. 14). Ironically, it is to these "unbelieving" disciples that Jesus assigns the great mission to proclaim the Good News or Gospel to all creation (v. 15).

Questions

1. How is your understanding of their great commissioning (v. 15) affected by the persistent disbelief displayed by the Eleven here in Mark 16 and throughout the Gospel?
2. What is the Good News to be proclaimed to the whole of creation (v. 15), and what connection, if any, does this have with the departure of Jesus?
3. Compare Mark 16:15–20 with Acts 1:1–11 and list both the similarities and differences between their respective accounts of the ascension.

4. How do you think the great commissions to the Eleven found in Mark 16:15 and in Acts 1:1–11 are connected to the ascension episode?

5. What connection is there between the longer ending of Mark, in particular verses 15–20, and the initial words of his Gospel (1:1)?

6. At the narrative level, identify as many "bumps" as possible in this longer ending of Mark that would indicate that it is a later addition to the Gospel.

7. In Acts, what texts from the First Testament might be echoed in Luke's description of the ascension of Jesus, and what does this finding suggest about the construction of this story?

Interpretive points

1. *Inauthentic, but canonical.* Both the shorter and longer endings to Mark's Gospel, though absent from the most important Greek manuscripts, including *Sinaiticus* and *Vaticanus*, have made the canon of the Church. This explains why they are generally incorporated in most Bibles. In addition to their absence from the Greek manuscript tradition, commentators have detected many elements that speak to their lack of authenticity. Style and vocabulary are not Markan, and, something that all readers can discover, there are a number of "bumps" that betray the secondary character of these verses. While the shorter ending contradicts the abrupt end of Mark 16:8, the longer ending does not even mention the name of Jesus and introduces Mary Magdalene as if she had not been mentioned before in the Gospel.

2. *Still failing disciples.* As readers will remember, the persistent failure of the twelve male disciples to grasp Jesus' message is one of the most important themes of Mark's Gospel. Today's Gospel reading omits the negative reaction of the Eleven to the reports from both Mary Magdalene and the two disciples (vv. 9–13), as well as Jesus' rebuke of their lack of faith in those who have already witnessed his resurrection (v. 14). One can only wonder if we are missing the message Mark is sending to his readers or community by omitting the fact that their failure persists even after Easter.

3. *A failing Church?* However difficult and delicate the task of figuring out the historical situation faced by the Markan community, certain things can be deduced from the disciples' difficulty to believe in the Risen Jesus. Sometime in the second century, if the manuscript tradition is to be trusted, we know that it was still no easy task for the leaders of the Church to proclaim Jesus' resurrection as part of the Good News to the whole world.

4. *Validating signs.* Few commentators have noted the slight discrepancy between verses 17–18 and 20. Both texts speak of "signs" accompanying and validating the missionary activity, but the subjects of that activity appear to be different in each text. According to the summary of verse 20, signs will accompany and confirm the missionary activity of the Eleven. It is to those who have believed the testimony of the original witnesses of the resurrection that signs will be granted as proofs of their success.

5. *I must go . . .* In the text from Acts 1, the mission of the Twelve is closely connected with the outpouring of the Spirit. For this to happen, however, Jesus must apparently go or depart, to use Johannine language. Mark, on the other hand, does not mention the Spirit at this point, but presents only Jesus' departure or ascension into heaven as following immediately upon his commissioning of the Eleven (v. 15).

Pastoral and homiletical notes

1. *Believing the word of another.* The persistence of the Eleven's skepticism with regard to the resurrection of Jesus, though omitted from today's Gospel selection, should not be overlooked when dealing with their commissioning and Jesus' ascension into heaven. The testimony of both Mary Magdalene and the two disciples does nothing to convince the Eleven, who need the intervention of the Risen Jesus himself to transform them into missionaries. Perhaps, faith in the resurrection should never be taken for granted? Then as now, it may be a constant struggle for many Christians.

2. *One single mystery.* The Church has adopted Luke's structure or time-line, presumably for theological and pedagogical reasons. As noted earlier, however, Christians should be made to understand that the ascension, like the upcoming Pentecost, is part and parcel of the one and same great mystery of Easter.

3. *Reporting the ascension.* Since both readings clearly were chosen for their "report" of the ascension of Jesus, they could well be used, with their differences and similarities, to instruct congregations on the rich diversity found in the Second Testament. If the overall message is one, the profiles are diverse, even within the work of one author, Luke!

4. *Where are the signs?* Christians should strive to proclaim the resurrection of Jesus, in and through their lives, in both words and deeds. If Mark is to be believed (vv. 16–17), preachers should have no difficulty finding "signs" of today that accompany those who believe in the Gospels' testimony of the resurrection of Jesus.

ORDINARY TIME

Interrupted by the long break of the Lenten season, Holy Week and the seven-week-long Easter season, Ordinary Time resumes after the feast of Pentecost with Trinity Sunday. In the *Roman Catholic Lectionary*, it begins with the feast of the Baptism of the Lord. The *Revised Common Lectionary* utilizes a different nomenclature for this lengthy series of Sundays, with few differences in their choice of readings. While the feast of the Baptism of the Lord follows the Christmas season in both lectionaries, the *Revised Common Lectionary* refers to the eight or nine Sundays before the Lent season as "Sundays after Epiphany." Also, the Sundays that follow the feast of Pentecost, including Trinity Sunday, are usually called "Sundays after Pentecost." In other lectionaries, starting with the sixth Sunday after Epiphany (the 6th Sunday in Ordinary Time in the *Roman Catholic Lectionary*), these Sundays may also be designated "Proper" 1, 2, 3, and so on.

In contrast with the other two years of the liturgical cycle, Ordinary Time in the year of Mark presents an important break during the summer months. For five consecutive Sundays (from the 17th to the 21st Sunday), the semi-continuous reading of Mark is replaced by readings from chapter 6 of John's Gospel on the Bread of Life. Whatever the reasons for such a move, and regardless of the importance of John 6, congregations will be deprived of a significant portion of the third major section of

Mark's Gospel. Readers and preachers will, therefore, do well to recall this section, if only to understand the few passages that have been retained by lectionaries.

One particular feature of the Sundays in Ordinary Time (or Proper in the *Revised Common Lectionary*) is the use of a First Testament text as first reading. As a general rule, in the *Roman Catholic Lectionary*, the First Testament text is chosen in reference to the Gospel reading for the day, acting as preparation for the Gospel message about Christ. The *Revised Common Lectionary* advocates an alternative reading taken from one or other book of the First Testament, read in semi-continuous mode, to offset what is seen as an overextension of the Christian connection to the First Testament.

9. THIRD SUNDAY IN ORDINARY TIME
THIRD SUNDAY AFTER EPIPHANY
Year B

<table>
<tr><td>Roman Catholic L
Jonah 3:1–5, 10
Mark 1:14–20</td><td>Revised Common L
Jonah 3:1–5, 10
Mark 1:14–20</td></tr>
</table>

PROCLAIMING THE GOOD NEWS OF GOD IN WORDS AND DEEDS
(MARK 1:14–20)

ON JONAH 3:1–5, 10

The story of Jonah's reluctance to preach God's mercy to the hated Assyrians of Nineveh is well known. In today's first reading, we hear of the prophet's final resignation to his prophetic task, of the surprising repentance of the whole city (vv. 5–9), and of God's own change of mind (v. 10).

Today's selection includes the only words spoken by Jonah in the entire book and they are words of judgment: "Forty days more, and Nineveh shall be overthrown!" Although his message neither calls for repentance, nor promises God's mercy, both are clearly the thrust of his intervention and what he fears most. For Jonah, justice, God's justice, demands the destruction of Nineveh! God's answer, however, is mercy. As the book ends, the real issue comes to the fore: like Nineveh, the prophet Jonah also is called to conversion. He knows of God's mercy (4:2) but, contrary to the people of Nineveh, does not yet really accept it (3:5).

ON MARK 1:14–20
Context

Mark's Gospel is traditionally divided into major sections, the first of which is Mark 1:14 to 3:6. This section is itself divided in two smaller units, 1:14–45 and 2—3:6. After calling his first four disciples, Jesus spends a long day in Capernaum, exorcising and healing people that are sick or possessed. This subsection is followed by Jesus' first controversies with religious authorities, ending with the beginning of a plot to destroy him (3:6). Throughout this first major section, the focus remains on Jesus, with the disciples—like the readers—on the sideline, observing.

Questions

1. In your view which comes first, "repentance" or "belief in the good news" (v. 15)?
2. At the narrative or story level (avoid the temptation of "psychologizing" the characters), what do you think prompts these would-be disciples to respond so quickly to Jesus' invitation to "come after him"?
3. What do you think is the purpose of these "call narratives" in the Gospel of Mark?

⊷ ❦ ❧ ⊶

4. How do you reconcile the first verse of the Gospel, "the good news of Jesus, Christ, Son of God" (1:1) with the statement that Jesus came to Galilee "proclaiming the good news of God" (1:14)?
5. How do you understand the word "repent" as used in this context?
6. Identify in the call narrative (1:16–20) what you perceive to be the main components of discipleship, and reflect on their implications.
7. What can we learn about the "genre" of these call narratives by comparing Mark 1:16–20 with the different versions of the same event in Luke (5:1–11) and John (1:35–42)?

Interpretive points

1. *Translation problems.* The problems facing translators should neither be minimized nor disregarded. Translators would be the first to acknowledge that to translate is to interpret. Three examples taken from verse 15, "the time is fulfilled, and the kingdom of God has come near," will show the complexity of any translation work. First, the most common translation might not sufficiently render the Greek emphasis on the *fulfillment* of the time and the *nearness or presence* of the sovereign rule of God. Although awkward, a more literal transla-

tion of the Greek, "*Fulfilled* [is] the time, *at hand* the kingdom of God," has the merit of showing where the emphasis should be placed. Second, it is not clear whether one should translate "the kingdom of God *is near* or is *at hand* (has already come)." How does your own Bible translate the phrase? Philology alone—the meaning and case of the Greek verb—cannot decide the issue. Also, one might conclude from a lack of scholarly unanimity on this issue that it cannot be decided from the context either. Whichever translation is chosen, the connection with Jesus' ministry must be respected.

A third and final translation problem in this phrase concerns the way the Greek *basileia* has been traditionally translated by the word "kingdom." The use of English words such as kingdom, reign, rule, sovereign rule, and so on, testifies not only to the richness of the Greek term, but also to the difficulty of encompassing its rich meaning into one single word. Also of concern, especially in our North American context, is people's increasing sensitivity to using words that are inclusive of everybody and devoid of any militaristic resonance. In this vein, there is perhaps more here to consider than a translation problem. What is this *basileia* of God about? It is not defined anywhere in Mark or in any other book from the Second Testament. Whatever resonance the term had for people of the first century CE, it was not apparently of much help to the disciples—if Acts 1:6 is to be believed—for understanding what it meant to Jesus. What do you think of Walter Wink's definition of the *basileia* as "God's domination-free society"?

2. *The disciples' story.* The story of the Call of the Disciples follows directly on the summary of Jesus' proclamation of the good news of God and can be seen as illustrating how the *basileia* of God affects people. In the words of Verner Kelber, "the Kingdom begins to involve people, it severs their ties to the past, puts them on the way and transplants them into a totally new mode of existence" (*Kingdom in Mark*, 15). In this sense, Mark's Gospel is not only the story of Jesus, Christ and Son of God. It is also the story of the disciples. They too, like the readers, will try to answer the question: Who is this man? This is where their story, their journey, also begins. Readers will soon discover that their story is quite different from what

one might have expected—especially after their quick response to the initial call from Jesus.

Pastoral and homiletical notes

1. *Thematic connection?* At first glance, repentance or the need to repent seems to be the only connecting theme between the reading from Jonah and the Gospel text. Even then, preachers may find themselves hard pressed to hold the two together. What is announced in Jonah 3:5 and further described in verses 6–9 (deleted from the lectionary selection) fits the more traditional meaning or understanding of repentance or penance. In calling for *metanoia* in Mark 1:15 (repent and believe in the good news), Jesus invites people, not to put on sack cloths, but to turn around, make a U-turn, change direction or orientation. This is the basic meaning of the Greek verb *metanoiein*, used here by Jesus.

2. *Converting to God's Ways.* In light of the above, it may be time to drop the word "repent" from our translations and choose another term more suited to the meaning of the Greek word. Such expressions as "change your ways, your heart and your mind," "turn (completely) around," or even "convert" may be preferable to the usual "repent" which the majority of our Christians identify with a call to repent from their sins. To enter the world of the *basileia*, would-be disciples will need more than to repent for their sins; they must, as the Gospel of Mark will show, experience *metanoia*. They must go to school— the school of Jesus—and learn about and embrace God's ways (Isa 55:8–9). This will not be a one-day trip, but a long and difficult journey with Jesus on the road to Jerusalem.

3. *Jonah and the disciples?* There is little interest in making of the "resisting" Jonah an anti-type of Jesus. It might be more profitable for preachers to draw a parallel between Jonah and the disciples. Called by God to be a prophet in one instance and to follow Jesus in the other, both will have difficulty entering the world of God—the *basileia*. Jonah has to discover that God's justice equals mercy, compassion, and magnanimity. As readers of Mark will soon discover, the

disciples are also in for a long and difficult journey. To read the narrative of their call as a theological construction in the present tense rather than a historical reminiscence would go a long way towards helping Christians get to the core of a story that concerns them too. They, like Jonah and the disciples, are called by Jesus to enter the world of the *basileia* of God and accept to be molded into disciples. There is a suitable theme for Advent!

Roman Catholic L	*Revised Common L*
Deuteronomy 18:15–20	Deuteronomy 18:15–20
Mark 1:21–28	Mark 1:21–28

TEACHING WITH AUTHORITY
(MARK 1:21–28)

ON DEUTERONOMY 18:15–20

Although seemingly directed to Israel before their entry into Canaan, these words of Moses are effectively addressed to the people already living in the land. Living among Canaanites, these people need help to stay away from "abhorrent practices" (18:9–14).

Read in that context, the divine promise to raise a prophet-like-Moses, who will speak the word of the Lord, raises the question of who this prophet will be. Is it a reference to the prophetic movement, so active throughout the monarchic period, and/or to a figure down the road in the eschatological future? Following the lead of many New Testament interpretations, but in spite of the warning that false prophets will die (18:20), Christians will identify this "prophet-like-Moses" with Jesus.

ON MARK 1:21–28
Context

Following the call of Simon, Andrew, James and John (1:16–20), Jesus comes to Capernaum—a city lying a few kilometers west of the Jordan at the north end of the lake of Galilee. Indications of time of day in the text have led scholars to speak here of "Jesus' day in Capernaum." It is in this city that Jesus begins his ministry. First, he exorcises a man from an unclean spirit (1:21–28), then cures Peter's mother-in-law (vv. 29–31), and concludes this long day with many other healing and exorcisms at sundown (vv. 32–39).

The day in Capernaum ends with Jesus telling Simon and the others: "Let us go on to the neighboring towns, so that I may proclaim the message there also; for that is what I came out to do" (1:38). So, as we move into the second half of this first chapter of Mark, readers are invited, together with the disciples, to observe, listen to, and learn from Jesus as he proclaims the good news. God's *basileia* breaks in above all in Jesus' actions.

Questions

1. Make a careful reading of the story and highlight (with different colors) any word or family of words that is used more than once. In light of this exercise, what do you think is the main focus of this passage?
2. Why do you think Jesus silences or "muzzles" the unclean spirit, even though the unclean spirit seems to speak the truth about him (1:25)?
3. Bearing in mind your findings to question one, what would you say the story is really about? What is at issue in this episode?

✦ ✦ ✦

4. Historically, who were the scribes and how are they characterized narratively, first here in 1:21–28, then in the rest of the Gospel?
5. Has the reader of Mark already been prepared, and if so where, for Jesus' victory over unclean spirits?
6. In light of Christian Churches' recent rejection of any teaching of contempt toward Judaism and the Jewish people, what do you make of this text's polemic against the scribes ("their" synagogues)?

Interpretive points

1. *Translation issue:* "Be silent, and come out of him!" (v. 25). The Greek verb, here translated as "be silent," means "to muzzle" or "to gag," a much stronger and graphic term than the "be silent" of most Bibles. The same verb will be used, and again translated as "be silent," in the story of the stilling of the storm in 4:39. While it apparently makes sense for Jesus, here in 1:25, to enjoin silence to an unclean spirit who speaks, the same command does not apply as well to the sea in 4:39. More importantly,

as we shall see later in our analysis of that story, in both instances the use of "muzzle" instead of "be silent" would guarantee that the second story—the stilling of the storm—is also read as an exorcism!

2. *Informal teaching?* In Mark, Jesus is predominantly a teacher and, as can be seen right here in our story, the spotlight on his teaching activity is turned on right at the start of his public ministry. His proclamation of the good news of God (1:14) will find one of its main expressions in teaching form. But how, then, should we explain the presence of so little formal teaching in this Gospel? Matthew and Luke's Gospels include much formal teaching material, while Mark supplies readers with little of the actual speaking content of Jesus' teachings.

3. *Teaching with authority.* Whatever the story is about, Jesus' teaching cannot be ignored, much less isolated from its interpretation. The exorcism (vv. 23–26) is bracketed between a summary of Jesus' teaching and the amazement of the people in the synagogue at his authority (vv. 21–22) and a conclusion about his "new teaching." According to verse 22, it is the way Jesus teaches "with authority," not his teaching, that surprises people. People react with amazement to the exorcism just performed by Jesus and speak of "a new teaching—with authority!" Casting out unclean spirits—healing—will be part of the new teaching of Jesus! As someone once wrote, when Jesus teaches in this Gospel, things happen!

4. *Misreading Jesus' identity.* Why would Jesus muzzle or silence unclean spirits (1:25, 34 and 3:11–12) when, for all intent and purpose, they speak the truth about him? Whatever truth these unclean spirits may possess about Jesus' true identity, Jesus seems to think that this is not the right time to speak it out. The rest of the Gospel will show that Jesus' identity as Christ, Son of God (1:1) cannot be understood and truly proclaimed (19:39) before his execution on the cross.

Pastoral and homiletical notes

1. *Reading Mark without anti-Semitism.* Here at the beginning of Jesus' teaching ministry we are presented with the potential, a potential al-

ready realized to an unacceptable degree in our world today, for the promotion of anti-Judaism and anti-Semitism. On this issue, the Gospel of Mark, compared with the other Gospels, gets generally little attention from scholars. It would be naïve, however, some would say ethically irresponsible, to ignore or simply dismiss Mark's polemic against the religious (Jewish) authorities. Such polemic may seem innocuous to many, but after Auschwitz, any sort of (Christian) stereotyping of individuals or categories of people of Jewish origin, has the potential of perpetuating a teaching that all Churches have now decisively rejected. In this respect, Mark's characterization of the scribes as having no "real" authority and his use of "their" synagogues create a picture of the Jewish institution and their authorities (together with the Pharisees) that has left its mark in Christian consciousness. After the *Shoah* and its impact upon the Christian world, this kind of stereotyping or stigmatizing has to be handled with great care. While one must avoid witch hunting, Christians must be informed of what many of us may still, though often unconsciously, harbor.

2. *Naming today's evil or unclean spirits.* Help Christians identify the evil or unclean spirits that possess people today and that need to be "exorcised" by the community.

3. *Teaching "with authority."* What does it mean for a Church to teach "with authority"? Looking at how Mark presents the teaching activity of Jesus—especially in the first half of the Gospel—might help to unravel this notion.

4. *Prophet-like-Moses.* One way to tie in with the first reading would be to say that if Jesus is indeed that prophet, his "teaching" includes healing, and so on.

11. Fifth Sunday in Ordinary Time
Fifth Sunday after Epiphany
Year B

Roman Catholic L	*Revised Common L*
Job 7:1–4, 6–7	Isaiah 40:21–31
Mark 1:29–39	Mark 1:29–39

More "New Teaching with Authority"
(Mark 1:29–39)

On Job 7:1–7

As it now stands, this passage from the book of Job sounds like the cry of despair of a person who suffers, who has lost everything, health, family, and wealth (Job 1–2). Yet, as the "remember" of verse 7 clearly shows, Job's lament is directed to God!

The book of Job—especially its central section—poses the problem of human suffering in a world governed by God. Through its main character, Job, it calls into question the traditional theology of retribution—defended so poorly by his friends and would-be comforters. Job's final conversation with God may not provide a satisfactory answer to the problem of suffering, but his rebellion is never condemned. Of all humans present, accuser and defenders, he is the one that has best spoken of God!

On Mark 1:29–39
Context

Mark's presentation of the first exorcism of Jesus as "a new teaching—with authority" should lead readers to view Jesus' subsequent healing activity in the same light. This first day in Capernaum concludes with the mention of a journey through Galilee, with Jesus pursuing his proclamation in words and actions (v. 39).

Questions

1. After Jesus heals the fever of Peter's mother-in-law, she serves Jesus and the disciples. What do you think of using Jesus' redefinition of service (10:45) as a lens for interpreting the "service" of Peter's mother-in-law in this story?
2. What do you think is, so early in the Gospel, the narrative and theological function of this summary of Jesus' activity (Mark 1:32–34)?
3. What do you make of Jesus' apparent lack of receptivity to the people's search for him (Mark 1:35–39)?

✦ ✦

4. Is there not some contradiction between the enthusiasm and fame that Jesus' healing activity generates among people and his refusal to let demons spell out his true identity?
5. What do you think is behind Jesus' withdrawal at this point to a deserted place to pray?
6. Does Mark show Jesus at prayer elsewhere in his Gospel, and how useful are these other occurrences for answering the first question?
7. "Everyone is searching for you" (v. 37). Who is "everyone" and, in searching for Jesus, what are all these people looking for?

Interpretive points

1. *Kitchen chores or Christian service?* As the very first woman to appear in Mark, Peter's mother-in-law has drawn the attention of feminist scholars. They were quick to recognize how such texts have been interpreted in order to maintain women's second-hand status both within the Church and society. This experience and analysis provides new perspectives, which cause many to read the Bible critically and with "suspicion" (known in the field as "hermeneutics of suspicion"). For example, one may ask why the names of the first four disciples called by Jesus are again mentioned in this story, but the person healed by Jesus has no name, known only through her relationship with Peter. The lack of a name for this woman is not unique. As we shall see later, many other women in Mark's Gospel—two of whom play significant roles in Jesus' life—are given no name.

    In this passage, the focus of feminist critics has centered on the Greek verb (*diakonei*), rendered by "to serve" in some translations or by "to wait on (them)" in others. Although its primary meaning is "service at table," this Greek verb has been interpreted in many different ways throughout the centuries. In Mark 10:45, Jesus himself uses this verb to describe his own ministry. He also uses it to teach the Twelve about how they are to exercise their authority (vv. 43–44). The question, which presents itself to us, here, is whether this term should be given the technical meaning of "service" as defined by Jesus in 10:45 and accepted within the Christian community by the time this Gospel was put into writing. Some scholars still hold that it should not, that it should be used in its more traditional sense. For example, Simon Légasse has recently suggested that we should "leave Peter's mother in law at home and to her chores" (*L'évangile de Marc*, vol. 1, 1997, 136), while Hugh Anderson suggests "serving at table remains the specific manner of discipleship for a woman." (*The Gospel of Mark*, 1981, 93). Feminist scholars reject these and similar readings. Standing strong on their experience as women, they no longer accept that a predominant ideology, patriarchal or otherwise, is capable of dictating the meaning of a text in all places and at all times. Should we interpret this story as simply one more report of a cure by Jesus or as a symbolic story of discipleship, open to each and every one of the readers?

2. *Ambiguity of miracles?* In their own distinctive way, the last two units of today's Gospel reading contrast the spectacular actions of Jesus with his efforts to ward off the danger of being misrepresented. It is as if Jesus cannot help from healing and exorcising, while at the same time doing everything possible to curtail the implications of this sort of activity. To explain this paradoxical attitude of Jesus, some will appeal to the Messianic Secret while others will ask why Jesus chooses, here and elsewhere, to withdraw from the crowds—to pray. Something is going on here that seems to trouble Jesus, and he needs to pause and reflect, and pray. In 1:12–13, readers learned that Satan in the wilderness tempted Jesus but, in contrast to Matthew and Luke, Mark was silent on the kind of temptations he faced. What concerns Jesus and prompts him to withdraw from the enthusiasm of the crowds?

Pastoral and homiletical notes

1. *Redefining "service"?* In light of the above considerations, preachers could use the story of the healing of Peter's mother-in-law to show their congregation what the "service" of this woman is about when interpreted through the lens of Jesus' redefinition of service in 10:45.

2. *Which passage?* The most difficult task for preachers, committed to preach on Sunday 5, might be to choose which of these little units to use for their reflections. Asking what constitutes "new teaching—with authority" in each unit might be a way to link all three episodes together.

3. *Learning from Jesus.* Just like their teacher, Jesus, the disciples were not inoculated against temptations of power (see especially Mark 8—10). In Gethsemane (14:38), Jesus will admonish them: "Keep awake and *pray* so that you may not come into the time of trial."

4. *Suffering to be respected.* By juxtaposing the reading from Job with this Gospel text, the lectionary seems to suggest that Jesus is the answer to people's suffering. This Christian view should not be used, however, to negate in any way or form Job's suffering and his questions. Preachers would also do well to remember Jesus' concern that his healing power might be misunderstood.

5. *A caring God.* Jesus cares for suffering people, like the God he proclaims cares, like the God that Job calls upon.

12. Sixth Sunday in Ordinary Time
Sixth Sunday after Epiphany
Year B

Roman Catholic L   *Revised Common L*

Leviticus 13:1–2, 45–46   2 Kings 5:1–14

Mark 1:40–45   Mark 1:40–45

Touching the Untouchable?
(Mark 1:40–45)

On Leviticus 13:1–2, 45–46

One of only two lectionary selections from the book of Leviticus, this passage is part of a major section of this book—called the purity code (11–15/16). This code is concerned with cases of ritual uncleanness and the means of regaining the state of purity. Four categories are singled out: clean and unclean animals, childbirth, leprosy or infectious diseases, and sexual uncleanness. Leviticus 13—14 deals with the unclean status of "lepers" among the Israelites. Today's passage, a concoction of the first and last two verses of Leviticus 13, suggests that the sickness referred to here is a temporary disorder that may disappear, not Hansen's incurable disease (the Hebrew term designates a variety of skin diseases) and that it is the priest's responsibility to determine whether this disorder is infectious or not. As long as this infectious disease afflicts this person, she or he is ritually unclean and isolated from both the worshipping community and society in general (vv. 44–46).

On Mark 1:40–45
Context

The episode of the purification of a leper follows a summary of Jesus' healing activity (1:32–34) and the news of his first preaching tour of Galilee (1:35–39). It closes the subsection that began in 1:16/21. With

74

Jesus' fame firmly established, people are now coming to him to be cured of their afflictions.

Questions

1. Do you feel comfortable with the way the biblical text categorizes people as *the* lepers, *the* sick, *the* sinners, *the* prostitutes, and so forth?
2. What do you think is behind Jesus' command to the leper to show himself to the priest: compliance with the Torah of Moses (Lev 13—14) or the leper's reinsertion to full membership in the community?
3. In what way could this healing be considered as another illustration of Jesus' new teaching with authority (1:29)?

✛— ✿ ✿ —✛

4. Why do you think Jesus adds "as a testimony to them" (1:44)?
5. What difference does it make that Jesus' response to the leper's request be motivated by compassion (pity), as most translations have it, or by anger, as others have it, and as is attested to in the Western (D) manuscript tradition?
6. Who do you consider the "lepers" of today's society?
7. Does the first reading connect to the Gospel text? If so, how?

Interpretive points

1. *Textual problem in verse 41.* A variant reading, found in the Western family of manuscripts (D), has Jesus acting out of anger rather than being moved with compassion. Of all major English Bible translations, only the *Revised English Bible* and the NRSV record this reading, making the text in the former and a footnote in the latter. The traditional reading has its critics even though it relies on strong manuscript evidence and appears to be supported by internal evidence (Mark shows Jesus acting out of compassion on two other occasions—in 6:34 and 8:2 with parallels in Matthew and Luke—but never out of anger). A case could be made for eliminating this questionable manifestation of anger in Jesus. A change by copyists from "moved with anger" (the most difficult reading) to "moved with pity" would be easier to understand than vice versa. The question also arises as to why Matthew and Luke—admittedly using Mark—would fail to

mention that Jesus was motivated by compassion from their version of this story when, as mentioned above, they keep it elsewhere.

What would make Jesus angry, the leprosy that has separated the man from his community, or the man himself who, in forcing Jesus' hand, now also makes him an untouchable, an outsider? This reading would make it easier to understand the sharp warning of Jesus (v. 43), all too often sanitized by translators. "Scolding" or "sternly ordering" him appears to suit better the undertone of violence carried by the Greek verb. (Bayard's *La Nouvelle Bible* has "en le rudoyant.") Could Jesus be trying to salvage his ministry, compromised by the fact that a leper has touched him? The narrator's indication that Jesus, following the man's rejection of his order, "could no longer go into town openly" (v. 45) might strengthen the case that Jesus will from now on be watched. In fact, Jesus faces his first challenge, starting in the very next story (2:1–12).

2. *Reinsertion in the community.* Jesus' decision to send the man to the priest for confirmation of his return to health can be variously explained. One obvious explanation is that the healing would not be complete without this person's reinsertion into the community. Without official appraisal and confirmation of his wellness, the man could not rejoin the community and attain "wholeness of being."

3. *Challenging the religious establishment?* Who are the people requiring evidence of the man's cure (note the shift to the plural: "as a testimony to *them*")? If they belong to the synagogues referred to earlier in Mark as *their* synagogues (1:23, 39), readers may be getting a glimpse of an existing conflict between this "Christian group" and these (Jewish) synagogues.

Pastoral and homiletical notes

1. *No objectifying people.* Over the past year, I have come to take great objection to labeling people as *the* sick, *the* lepers, *the* poor, *the* downtrodden. In my mind speaking of persons in this way accomplishes two things: It objectifies them and distances us from the real issues at hand. My hope would be that we give thought to the words we speak and to how they affect those we seek to help.

2. *What about "wholeness"?* To speak of the man's return to "wholeness of being" will raise questions for some. A friend of mine would immediately question my use of this word (she already has), challenging me, on behalf of a great number of people out there, to imply that they are not whole persons. It is as if wholeness and impediments, physical or otherwise, were incompatible. She has a point.

3. *Healing one's attitudes.* Full reinsertion in the community, social, religious, and cultural, ought to be part and parcel of any healing process. But for people that have been cut from their community or society, a change of attitude within the society or community might be the only way to bring the healing process to fruition. This is where healing, most of the time, will be needed!

13. Seventh Sunday in Ordinary Time
Seventh Sunday after Epiphany
Year B

<table>
<tr><td>Roman Catholic L</td><td>Revised Common L</td></tr>
<tr><td>Isaiah 43:18–19, 20–22, 24c–25</td><td>Isaiah 43:18–25</td></tr>
<tr><td>Mark 2:1–12</td><td>Mark 2:1–12</td></tr>
</table>

Forgiveness of Sins in the Community
(Mark 2:1–12)

On Isaiah 43:18–25

One of the objectives of Second Isaiah—this anonymous exilic prophet—was to convince the exiles that God, Creator and Savior, was overseeing the end of their tribulations and their impending return to the homeland. As the first verses of this reading will show, God—the speaker throughout—is about to accomplish this homecoming.

Today's selection can be divided into three parts. Two divine promises bracket a lament. In the first part, God invites the exiles to focus on the "new Exodus" that is about to take place. For the occasion, the inhabited desert separating Babylon from Israel will be made into hospitable land for God's chosen people (vv. 18–21). Then, in a rather surprising turn of events, God is found lamenting over the continuous unworthiness of the people (vv. 22–24), only to promise, in the end, that Israel's sins will be forgiven (v. 25). Jacob/Israel have done nothing to deserve it, but their God is a merciful God.

On Mark 2:1–12
Context

In Mark 1:21–45 Jesus has provided new teaching with authority, over unclean spirits, all kind of illnesses, fever, even leprosy, a teaching that is accepted enthusiastically by the people. In the next subsection (2:1—3:6), a drastic shift takes place. While Jesus continues to teach with authority, his authority is suddenly being questioned, challenged, and even attacked. A new mood sets in. Conflicts arise with the religious establishment—chiefly, scribes and Pharisees—over such issues as forgiveness of sins, open table, fasting, and "work" during the Sabbath. The controversies are deadly serious, involving more than differences of opinion. Two conflicting world views collide, and by the time we reach the end of the section (3:6), the Pharisees have joined Herod's people to devise a way to put Jesus to death.

Questions

1. Whose faith brings about Jesus' benevolent action towards the paralyzed man?
2. What do you make of Jesus' surprising switch to the forgiveness of sins in his response to the paralyzed man (2:5b)?
3. Does the narrative add anything to the characterization of the scribes in 1:22?
4. What is the major contrast between Jesus and the scribes he encounters here over their attitude towards the paralyzed man?

⊹⊱ ❦ ❧ ⊰⊹

5. What leads the scribes to accuse Jesus of blasphemy?
6. Does the narrative attribute authority (Gk *exousia*) to Jesus to forgive sins?
7. Considering that this passage refers to "the Son of Man" as encompassing more than the person of Jesus, do you think it has anything to say on where the authority to forgive sins "on earth" resides in our world today?
8. Scholars generally call this narrative a "pronouncement story." Is the expression helpful to determine what the story is really about?

Interpretive points

1. *There is more here than a miracle story.* Jesus' response to the faith of the "community" (v. 5a) needs explanation. One would expect Jesus to say right away, as he does in verse 9, "Stand up, take your mat and walk."

Why does Jesus refer here to "forgiveness of sins" instead? Readers of Mark will again encounter a similar shift in the story of the encounter of Jesus with a Syrophoenician woman in 7:27. As a result, these stories are forever altered, taking on a new twist. In Mark 7, it is the question of the salvation of the Gentiles that suddenly bursts into view, while, here in Mark 2, it is no less the crucial issue of the forgiveness of sins that now takes center stage. In both instances, the "miracle story" has become, rhetorically speaking, the vehicle for some important teachings.

2. *Forgiveness of sins?* Scholars are divided on how to interpret the surprising shift of Jesus to forgiveness of sins. Are readers required to know of the connection between sickness and sin—once a dogma in Jewish theology—to explain the twist in the story? If so, this subtext cannot be ignored—no matter how offensive such a view might sound to our modern sensitivities. For reasons that, in my judgment, seem to stem more from hermeneutical than exegetical considerations, some recent scholars may be too quick in dismissing the traditional connection between sickness and sin, calling instead for a general reference from Jesus to the sinful human condition.

3. *The role of faith.* This miracle story ends on the usual note of amazement (v. 12b). One may wonder, however, at the silence of the text on the scribes' response to this spectacular demonstration by Jesus. This peculiar omission raises the question of the role of faith in our understanding and acceptance of the authority of Jesus. It is this faith, the faith of the community that calls forth this healing authority and compels Jesus to reach out to the paralytic.

4. *Assuming God' authority.* As official teachers and interpreters of the Torah, the scribes have the responsibility to ensure that the Torah be correctly understood, including their understanding of God. In declaring the man forgiven of his sins, Jesus appropriates God's authority to forgive sins (Exod 34:6; Isa 43:5 and 44:2), and, in their eyes, threatens "the system" that they are charged with preserving. Jesus is here assuming an authority that belongs to God alone.

Pastoral and homiletical notes

1.   *The forgiving faith of the community?* Jesus' surprising action should not be divorced from the community's conduct towards the man ("When Jesus *saw* their faith . . ."). The man would still be in a state of both physical and spiritual paralysis, had not the community's faith compelled Jesus to act. This Markan passage confers a definitive role to the community in the man's restoration to life. What role do you see our communities playing in the forgiveness of sins?

2.   *Who is the blasphemer?* There is much talk in our time of blasphemy, of sacrilege, irreverence, disrespect, of dissent, unorthodoxy, revisionism, and so on. One may wonder where Jesus would stand in this array of voices, all defending what they believe is the right way to express the Gospel. Which system is being defended and whose interests are being fostered? The "Jesus" and the "scribes" may not be so easily discernable in our world as they are in this passage. Symbolically, Jesus and the scribes can represent any one person or group today. This story reminds us to be very careful distinguishing who's whom and where our loyalties should lay.

14A. Eighth Sunday in Ordinary Time
Year B

Roman Catholic L
Hosea 2:14, 15b, 19–20
Mark 2:18–22

Conflict over Fasting . . .
(Mark 2:18–22)

On Hosea 2:14–20

Although the book of Hosea is known for its language of love and compassion, judgment remains at the forefront of the prophetic message. The relationship between Yahweh and Israel has gone sour and the latter are about to suffer the consequences of their infidelity. Yet, there is hope for Israel. The book displays over and over this great paradox of God's implacable anger against Israel's infidelity and of the divine tenderness and love for this unfaithful people. For some, its sequence and connection might be problematic.

This pattern is well illustrated in Hosea 1—3 where the author uses the metaphor of the "husband and (unfaithful) wife" to describe God's difficult and painful relationship with Israel. Today's selection, taken from the central piece of this first section of the book, leaves out the dreadful description of the punishment of the unfaithful wife/Israel—the apparent precondition to God's future restoration of the relationship. A difficult passage has been omitted, but to what purpose?

On Mark 2:18–22
Context

The third of five controversies that make up the subsection of Mark 2:1–3:6, today's Gospel selection addresses the question of the disciples' practice of fasting or lack of fasting. In all probability, these controversy stories reflect early Christian debates utilizing statements (or pronouncements) of Jesus to legitimate or validate practices and views upheld by the community—hence the name of "pronouncement story" given to this type of accounts.

Some scholars have suggested a concentric or chiastic structure for Mark 2:1–3:6, with 2:18–22 acting as center of the "chiasm." In this type of structure (A, B, C, A^1, B^1 with each letter standing for an episode), the middle unit—here symbolized by C—is expected to carry the main focus or climax of the whole frame. For these scholars, Mark 2:18–22 becomes a more crucial text than many exegetes are ready to concede.

Questions

1. What do you think verses 18–20 are about, the issue of fasting or the significance of the rite?
2. What do you think fasting means for the disciples of Jesus?
3. Are verses 18–20 and 21–22 connected and, if so, in what way? Why would a Bible translation such as the NRSV separate the two units only in Mark, while keeping them joined in Matthew and Luke?

⊷ ❦ ❧ ⊶

4. Does Mark, or any other of the Gospels, have anything more to say about fasting practices among the disciples of John and the Pharisees?
5. What do you think the whole passage is about?
6. Does the language used in the two little parables have the potential of promoting "supersessionism," and if so can you think of ways to counteract its effect?

Interpretive points

1. *Not fasting, like their Teacher.* This controversy over fasting raises two very distinct questions. Why do the disciples of Jesus not fast, like John and the Pharisees' own disciples, and what makes Jesus' departure a "time indicator" that the time for fasting has now come? In his answer, Jesus uses the metaphor of the bridegroom to explain both the present and future attitudes of his disciples towards fasting. Besides the remarkable claim that the metaphor implies for Jesus, it also de-

scribes his ministry as a wedding feast with the bridegroom present. If we are to believe what Matthew and Luke tell us, Jesus and John were two very different "prophets." As for the Pharisees, again according to Luke (18:12), they fasted twice a week, on Tuesdays and Thursdays. Jesus, according to Matthew and Luke (but not Mark), might have fasted 40 days and nights following his baptism, but he was clearly not the ascetic type for the majority of his contemporaries. One consequence of this is that, unlike the disciples of John and the Pharisees, Jesus' own disciples could not emulate their teacher, be modeled upon Jesus' practice; they could not revert to specific teachings or attitudes of Jesus.

2. *Fasting as memorial?* The answer to the second question is more elusive. Why will Jesus' departure (when the bridegroom is taken away) inaugurate the time to fast for the disciples? What is the connection between Christian fasting and the death of Jesus? Could fasting practice—Christian fasting that is—have something to do with "remembering" the death and resurrection of Jesus until he returns? When Mark refers to the necessity for the disciples to fast "on that day," could he point in a rather oblique way, as it has been suggested, to a liturgical use of fasting—a "memorial" of the Christ event, until he returns?

3. *Christian fasting.* Apparently, this specific relation to Christ is what makes Christian fasting practice different from the practices of both John and the Pharisees' disciples. It would thus be the function of the next two short parables—about the necessity of sewing a piece of unshrunk cloth on a new cloak and putting new wine into fresh wineskins—to inform readers of the different meaning of Christian fasting.

Pastoral and homiletical notes

1. *Connecting to Hosea 2?* It is not clear to me what the connection is, if any, between this Gospel text and the first reading from Hosea 2. It might be easier for users of the *Revised Common Lectionary* to find a way to connect these two readings. The episode of the Call of Levi and of Jesus' association with Tax Collectors (2:13–17)—not retained

in the *Roman Catholic Lectionary*—could be exploited as one example of God's loving attitude towards "unfaithful people." However, since there seems to be little connection between the two pericopes, they may have to ignore the discussion over fasting.

2. *There is fasting and fasting!* It strikes me that this text from Mark could have been chosen for the First Sunday of Lent in Year B (the year of Mark). One reason for this omission might well be that this Christological presentation of Christian fasting would not fit the kind of fasting prescribed for the Lenten Period. This, indirectly, would confirm our interpretation of this passage.

3. *Christologically-oriented practice.* Given the ever-present danger that our Christian texts or discourses be seen as disregarding the value of other religious practices—those of John and the Pharisees—I would suggest to emphasize the Christological meaning of the Christian practice rather than its "newness"—as opposed to older ones.

14B. EIGHTH SUNDAY AFTER EPIPHANY
Year B

Revised Common L
Hosea 2:14–20
Mark 2:13–22

CONFLICT OVER RECONCILIATION WITH "TAX COLLECTORS AND SINNERS"
(MARK: 2:13–22)

ON HOSEA 2:14–20

For the study guide on Hosea 2:14–20, see chapter 14a.

ON MARK 2:13–22

Context

The stories of Jesus' call of Levi (vv. 13–14) and his "dubious" association with "tax collectors and sinners" (vv. 15–17) follow the healing of the paralytic man. It is the second of five controversy stories that make up the subsection of Mark 2:1—3:6.

Questions

1. After 1:16–20, what do you think is the narrative purpose of this second "call narrative"?
2. How do you interpret Jesus' association with "tax collectors and sinners"? What do you think of such an association?
3. What do you make of this division between righteous and sinners in verse 17? Is this not a potentially dangerous construct? Who are, today, the "righteous" and the "sinners" in our faith communities?

86

4. What do you think of the combination "tax collectors and sinners"?
5. How is one to explain such opposition from people of Pharisaic faith to Jesus' association with sinners?
6. What is your definition of the Pharisees and where does such a definition come from? Do you know of any documents from your church denomination that deal with the Christian depiction of the Pharisees?
7. What is (really) at issue in this episode? Which barriers is Jesus breaking?

Interpretive points

1. *Breaking barriers in the name of the* basileia. Tax collectors and (public) sinners were barred from the worshipping community: either because their occupation was unacceptable or their status reprehensible. For all purposes, they were cut off from their faith community. By inviting one tax collector to follow him, even sharing meals with his friends, Jesus cuts through barriers set up by the purity system. Jesus continues to teach "as one having authority, and not as the scribes" (1:22), but his authority is now questioned. Why and by whose authority is Jesus breaking open the "system" (2:16)? In the name of the *basileia* of God and who can censure God?

2. *Rehabilitating the Pharisees.* Mark 2:16 refers to the Pharisees for the first time, using a rather unusual expression, "the scribes of the Pharisees," which incidentally both Matthew (9:11) and Luke (5:30) have corrected. The Pharisees are mentioned several more times in this subsection (2:1—3:6)—not to mention the rest of the Gospel—questioning Jesus, watching him, and finally plotting his death with Herod's people (3:6). The pattern is already set up: from now up to the passion, they will model the main opposition to Jesus.

    Readers, especially Christian readers, know the Pharisees well—perhaps too well. They are known as the "bad boys" of the Gospels and, unfortunately, also for preachers. Historical research over the last forty years has unearthed a picture of the Pharisees that is very different from that commonly presented in the Gospels. The Pharisees are now viewed as a religious group whose primary goal was to invite people to be holy as their God was holy. And it is to achieve this goal that they developed what has been called a "hedge" around the Torah—to ensure that the latter would be fully observed. This is in sharp contrast to their characterization as hypocrites in the Gospels. According to recent scholarship the Pharisees were for all purposes holy people striving to respond to their God's call to holiness and bring God's people along.

The Guidelines and Suggestions for Implementing the Conciliar Declaration "Nostra Aetate"—a Roman Catholic document published in 1974—cautions preachers to handle with care the term "Pharisees" (and the expression "the Jews" in John's Gospel). Interestingly, in the same document, Christians are challenged, not only to give more time to the study of Judaism, but also to learn how the Jews define themselves. In other words, it is no longer ethically responsible to keep talking about the Jewish people and their faith, about the Pharisees and other Jewish groups and institutions, as if the *Shoah* had never happened.

Pastoral and homiletical notes

1. *The Revised Common Lectionary* selection for Proper 3 includes both the episode of Jesus' association with tax collectors and the discussion over fasting. The difference in topics will force preachers to make a choice between the two pericopes. On the other hand, the Call of Levi and Jesus' association with Tax Collectors (2:13–17)—not retained in the *Roman Catholic Lectionary*—could be exploited as one example of God's loving attitude towards "unfaithful people" (the Hosea reading).

2. *A friend of tax collectors and sinners.* Tax collectors and (public) sinners do not seem to follow Jesus because of his calling one of them to become a disciple. According to Mark 2:15, many were associating with Jesus before Levi is ever called to follow him! Moreover, why are we so quick to assume that Jesus' association with them implies a change of heart, conversion to discipleship? True, this may be how Luke understands it ("I have come to call not the righteous, but sinners *to repentance*"—5:32), but one Gospel—Luke in this case—cannot be used to interpret the text of another. On this question, Mark is mute—

which leaves readers free to speculate on these public sinners' motives for following Jesus. In Jesus, could they be simply welcoming a friend? According to both Matthew and Luke, this is how Jesus is labeled by Pharisees and scribes: "The Son of Man has come eating and drinking, and you say, 'Look, a glutton and a drunkard, *a friend* of tax collectors and sinners' " (Luke 7:34)!

3. *They should be in our midst.* It may be an interesting exercise for preachers to explain who (public) sinners and tax collectors were at the time of Jesus, but it should not deter them from helping their congregation to identify today's "tax collectors and sinners." Whatever their identity, they are either present in the community, becoming a source of reflection on the breaking of the *basileia* "among us," or they are not in attendance, then compelling the community to wonder why such people are excluded from their midst. Either way, the text of Mark will be occasion for reflection and perhaps also conversion.

4. *Identifying today's "righteous people."* Yet, the big question arising from the text of Mark is not the identity of the tax collectors and sinners. These people are not the problem; the scribes of the Pharisees or what they represent are! Could they be those "righteous people" who have no need of a physician?

5. *Subverting the tradition.* A church—someone has written—which draws a line between sinners and righteous runs the risk of siding with the scribes (of the Pharisees).

6. *Speaking of the Pharisees.* As rule of thumb, whenever and wherever you refer to the Pharisees, make sure to include yourself and your congregation among them!

15. Ninth Sunday in Ordinary Time
Proper 4
Year B

Roman Catholic L   *Revised Common L*

Deuteronomy 5:12–15   Deuteronomy 5:12–15

Mark 2:23—3:6   Mark 2:23—3:6

Lord of the Sabbath
(Mark 2:23—3:6)

On Deuteronomy 5:12–15

Today's first reading—taken from the book of Deuteronomy—provides a reformulation of the commandment to observe the Sabbath (Exod 20:8–11). While the command is similar in both versions, the motives for its observance are different. In Exodus 20, the people are called to observe this weekly holy day *in remembrance* of God's rest after creation. However, here in the book of Deuteronomy, their observance of this day will be, instead, *in remembrance* of their liberation from Egypt by the mighty hand of God (v. 15). It is not immediately clear how this new motive relates to the command for every one—people and livestock alike—to rest on this day. Were people to understand this Sabbath, or rest for all, as the "great equalizer" or as a reminder of their responsibility to foster a world devoid of exploitation or oppression?

The Sabbath is, still today, one significant identity marker for Jews. Because of its religious significance and the penalties that its violation brings about, "a large corpus of legal interpretation developed among Jewish groups to determine just what constituted 'work' or other violations of the Sabbath law" (Donahue-Harrington, *Mark*, 110–111). Interestingly, while there are no less than 39 violations explicitly mentioned in the *Shabbat tractate* (from the *Mishnah*), neither the plucking of grain, nor the treatment of illness, mentioned in our Markan reading of today, is specifically named.

ON MARK 2:23—3:6
Context

Two Sabbath episodes—a teaching about the Sabbath (2:23–28) and the Man with a Withered Hand (3:1–6)—conclude the controversy section that began in 2:1. That last healing, apparently taking place in the very same synagogue where Jesus has performed his first exorcism (1:21; cf. 3:1), also brings to a close the first major division of Mark's Gospel (1:21—3:6). Although the conflict with the Pharisees has been intensifying throughout the last chapter, readers will nevertheless be surprised to hear in 3:6 that a plot is already under way to get rid of Jesus.

Questions

1. What do you know of the Jewish Sabbath and where does such knowledge come from?
2. Of the many statements made by Jesus in these two stories, which one would you list as the most important and how does this statement contribute to your understanding of these stories?
3. Do you think Jesus' understanding of, or challenge to, the Sabbath institution is of any relevance for our own institutions today?

❈ ❈ ❈

4. What do you make of Jesus' response (Mark 2:27) to the objection from the Pharisees, and why do you think Matthew (12:8) and Luke (6:5) both choose to omit this statement?
5. What do you think that Jesus has done that would cause the Pharisees to conspire with the Herodians to destroy him?
6. In a post-holocaust era, why do you think these two passages need to be handled with care?

Interpretive points

1. *Lord of the Sabbath.* For most commentators, the issue underlying both episodes is not the Sabbath itself but a different understanding of its purpose and observance. More specifically, it is the purpose of both these Markan stories to teach that the Sabbath was made for the benefit of people and not vice versa. The problem with this view is its

total lack of biblical foundation. Nowhere in the Bible is this "compassionate aspect" of the Sabbath observed. Rather, the focus is on rest and on the penalties for breaking Sabbath. Contrary to Jesus' appeal to Genesis 1—2 to ground his argument on the issue of divorce (Mark 10), his apparent reinterpretation of the Sabbath finds no ground in Scripture. However, as we have witnessed in our First Testament reading, this is not uncommon, nor unlawful. So, one may ask, what prompts Pharisees and Herodians to join hands in plotting the death of Jesus?

The authorities' plot to get rid of Jesus is not for his breaking of or reinterpreting of the Sabbath, but because of what is implied by his actions. As we said earlier, Jesus' radical reinterpretation has no explicit biblical foundation. It rests entirely on his authority—his *exousia*. In 2:5, Jesus, of his own authority, has declared the sins of the paralytic man forgiven; here, he is reinterpreting the Sabbath. He does this in a way that threatens the "system" and its keepers. This threat to the system needs to be removed. Jesus has become a serious liability (3:6).

2. *Superseding the Sabbath?* The debate around the Sabbath takes on a different color when viewed in the context of Mark's community. If the Sabbath had already been replaced in that community by the first day of the week (Mark 16:1–2), why would the former need to be reinterpreted at all? The Sabbath may not be explicitly condemned or rejected in these passages, but, according to the Markan Jesus, for all intents and purposes, it is now robbed of its essence. The danger inherent in this interpretation, however, cannot be ignored today. Christian understanding and interpretation of the Sabbath is only one and, though valid, cannot in any way invalidate Jewish understanding or interpretation of their Sabbath. (See the recent document of the PBC, *The Jewish People and Their Holy Scriptures in the Christian Bible.*)

Pastoral and homiletical notes

1. *Defining the Sabbath rightly.* Whatever reading is adopted of these two stories, some caution will be needed around the issue of the Sabbath. Preachers and catechists should avoid anything that might perpetuate

the view that the Jewish Sabbath has now been made obsolete. On this issue, they will especially recall the suggestion from the Vatican *Guidelines and Suggestions for Implementing the Conciliar Declaration "Nostra Aetate"* (December 1974):

> They must strive to acquire a better knowledge of the basic components of the religious tradition of Judaism; they must strive to learn by what essential traits the Jews define themselves in the light of their own religious experience (Introduction, par. 6).

2. *Staying away from supersessionism.* On this same issue, the treatment of the Sabbath in the new 1993 *Catechism* of the Roman Catholic Church needs to be handled with care. While good on its biblical origin and its contemporary meaning (par 2168–2172), it does little to reverse the view that the Sabbath—having found its fulfillment in the day of Lord—now belongs to "the old order of things" (par 2175 and 2190).

3. *Sunday observance.* In appearing to trivialize the many prohibitions devised over time to protect people from breaking the Sabbath, the first story seems to reduce Sabbath observance to a set of rules or regulations, and so devalue the Sabbath itself. Should this danger help us to take a hard look at our own Sunday observance?

4. *System threatened.* What happens in our own Churches when the "system" is threatened from within or without? How do you think Mark's Jesus would be received in our Christian Churches of today?

16. Tenth Sunday in Ordinary Time
Proper 5
Year B

<table>
<tr><td align="center">Roman Catholic L
Genesis 3:9–15
Mark 3:20–35</td><td align="center">Revised Common L
Genesis 3:8–15
Mark 3:20–35</td></tr>
</table>

Jesus' New Family
(Mark 3:20–35)

On Genesis 3:8–15

If read metaphorically, as the rest of Genesis 1—11, today's excerpt from Genesis 3 can provide valuable insights concerning the human condition. The ideal world of Genesis 2 gives way to the real world of Genesis 3—a world we all know too well. In place of a completely peaceful and harmonious world, the fall introduces disharmony between God and God's creation (Gen 3:1–7). In this new order of things, human relationships are also affected. Naked but not ashamed (2:25), the man and the woman now seek to hide from each other (3:7).

In today's reading, the disharmony introduced by the fall is evident. Adam is now afraid of God and wants to hide. He then passes the blame to the woman who in turn blames the serpent. Now that both humans have failed to take responsibility for their actions, the "trial" can begin. In today's excerpt we do not hear of the curse placed on the man or the woman, but only of that placed on the serpent.

On Mark 3:20–35
Context

Since most of chapters 3 and 4 are excluded from the lectionary, preachers will do well to get a sense of the general context in which the few stories that have been retained, occur. To provide a context to better understand Mark 3:20–35, we must go back to what is generally viewed as the second major section of the Gospel of Mark (3:7—6:6a). This section is framed by two stories of opposition to Jesus: from his relatives and the scribes (3:20–35) and from the people of his home village (6:1–6a). It also includes two large subsections that bracket these two incidents: Jesus' teaching in parables (4:1–34) and four mighty acts that occur in the context of a long sea journey (4:35—5:43).

The immediate narrative context of 3:20–35 is a transitional "summary report" (3:7–12), simultaneously concluding the first major part of the Gospel and providing a "transition" to the next section. With people coming to Jesus from all parts of the country and beyond, he is forced to look for a "way out" (first mention of the boat) because of the crushing pressure of the crowds. Even the unclean spirits are milling around with their unwelcome claims to Jesus' identity. The next episode sees Jesus appointing twelve of his disciples to be with him, eventually sending them out to preach and giving them authority to cast out demons (a commissioning to occur in chapter 6:7–13). Almost in the same breath, as Jesus surrounds himself with this core group of disciples, readers learn of the mounting opposition to him, some coming from rather surprising sources—his own family.

Questions

1. Name the two charges leveled against Jesus in this passage (3:20–35) and indicate who makes them.
2. What do you make of these two different translations of 3:21?

    When his *relations* heard of this, *they* set out to take charge of him; *they* said "He is out of his mind." (*New Jerusalem Bible*) When his *family* heard it, *they* went out to restrain him, for *people* were saying, "He has gone out of his mind." *(New Revised Standard Version)*

    *   Compare your own Bible translation with the two shown above.
    *   Do you think 3:31–35 might be of any help in solving this problem?
    *   Does Mark 6:1–6b offer any clue on how to interpret this passage?
3. What do you think is the real issue in Mark 3:22–29 and what do you make of Jesus' argument in verses 23–27?

⊱ ❦ ⊰

4. Do you recognize Mark's favorite "sandwich" or "intercalation" technique in this passage and what might be the function of such an arrangement?

5. What distinguishes Jesus' attitude towards his family, here in Mark 3:21, 30–35, from his position in Luke's Gospel (8:19–21)?

6. What do you think makes the claim that Jesus is possessed with an "unclean spirit" a blasphemy against the Holy Spirit (28–30)? Do you believe there is such a thing as an "unforgivable sin"?

Interpretive points

1. *Sandwich technique.* The bracketing or framing of one story by another is a favorite Markan literary technique. Here for example, an accusation by the scribes from Jerusalem that Jesus is in league with Beelzebub is framed by the two halves of a story of how Jesus is also misunderstood by members of his own family. The purpose of this technique would be for the two stories to explain each other. This favorite technique of Mark can be found again, most explicitly, in 5:21–43; 6:7–31; and 11:12–25.

2. *Translation problem.* As your research will have shown, not all Bibles agree on whom, of the people or his own family, considers Jesus "out of his mind." Although grammatically possible, if not plausible, the first reading remains unusual, not the least because readers have been given no "cause to think that people in general thought Jesus insane" (France, 167). One is left wondering, therefore, if this peculiar translation is not an attempt to remove the potentially offensive character of verse 21. This seems all the more probable when—thanks to Mark's framing technique—readers learn in 3:30–35 that among them is Jesus' own mother! Ironically, this same potential discomfort with putting the blame on the family of Jesus may have motivated the change from "his relatives/family" to "the scribes and the rest" in some manuscripts.

3. *Let Mark be Mark!* Readers who may have found our previous discussion somewhat discomforting should remember that Mark, unlike Matthew and Luke, has no "birth or infancy narratives." Could it be the reason why both evangelists have eliminated from their narratives

this "negative" comment attributed to Jesus' family? In all likelihood, Mark (the first written Gospel?) did not know of any positive traditions about the family of Jesus!

4. *Metaphorical house?* It is not clear whether the house to which Jesus is said to go (v. 19) is a reference to Jesus' own home (as the NRSV suggests) or refers to the metaphorical house which in Mark is frequently used, not only to divide outsiders from insiders, but also a place where the latter will benefit from Jesus' instruction or revelation (as here in 3:21 and 3:31–35).

Pastoral and homiletical notes

1. *Family ties and discipleship.* Jesus' word about his new family is not the only one in Mark to touch family connections. In Mark 10:28–31, discipleship will involve choices that may impact family ties. Mark 13:12 raises the specter of family betrayals in time of persecutions. These are "hard words" that need to be handled with care. God speaks in mysterious ways to peoples' hearts, but as Genesis 3 reminds us, betrayals and disruptions in human relationships can be a painful heartfelt matter.

2. *Doing God's will.* Jesus' statement that "whoever does the will of God is [his] brother and sister and mother" (v. 35) demands some explanation. Although nowhere in Mark is there an explicit description or definition of the will of God, I would suggest we look at Jesus' prayer in Gethsemane for what doing God's will might be all about (14:36). This final prayer makes sense only in light of Jesus' whole life and the choices he made all along. These choices were to remain faithful to his conscience and his God and, in the end, this is what finally caused him to be killed.

3. *Connection with Genesis 3?* The connection between these two readings is not obvious. The "demonic," a clear misrepresentation of the serpent, does not suffice as a connecting link. I would suggest that the theme of a propensity for disharmony in creation, human relationships included, might prove more helpful. Why, one may ask, do not only the scribes from Jerusalem but also Jesus' own family misunderstand and let him down?

17. Eleventh Sunday in Ordinary Time
Proper 6
Year B

Roman Catholic L	*Revised Common L*
Ezekiel 17:22–24	Ezekiel 17:22–24
Mark 4:26–34	Mark 4:26–34

Hidden, Insignificant, but a Sure Thing
(Mark 4:26–34)

On Ezekiel 17:22–24

This passage forms the conclusion to the long allegory of the two eagles in 17:1–10. As the following interpretation shows (17:11–21), the prophet Ezekiel—already exiled in Babylon—experiences deep concerns about the political situation in Israel. Like Jeremiah before him, he seems unhappy about King Zedekiah's futile rebellion against the Babylonian yoke and his furtive look towards Egypt. Alliance with Egypt against the great Babylonian eagle cannot but bring catastrophe for Judah. Today's selection—which follows immediately upon the announcement of the Pharaoh's defeat at the hands of God (vv. 19–21)—looks towards a future ruled by God, the Lord of History. Returning to the initial imagery of the cedar and sprig, the prophet makes not only a theological reading of this political event, but resolutely takes the side of Israel. God's victory over the "high tree" and the promising return to the Davidic dynasty (making high the low tree) will ensure that the name of the Lord is exalted.

On Mark 4:26–34
Context

As the concentric structure below shows, the two seed parables and the statement about Jesus' general practice of teaching the crowds in parables

(4:26–34) form the concluding segment of what is generally referred to as Jesus' parabolic discourse (4:1–34).

A. Introduction (4:1–2)
   B. Parable of the Sowings (4:3–9)
      C. Reason for Speaking in Parables (4:10–12)
         D. Allegory of the Seeds (4:13–20)
      C^1. Enigmatic Sayings (4:21–25)
   B^1. Seeds Parables (4:26–32)
A^1. Conclusion (4:33–34)

In 4:1–2, readers learn that Jesus is back by the lakeside, "teaching" crowds of people "many things in parables." Immediately following this introduction, we find, first, the parable of the Sower or of the (Four) Sowings (vv. 3–8); second, the reason for Jesus' speaking in parables (10–12); and third, an explanation or "allegorization" of the parable of the Sower (vv. 14–20). The passage for today's Gospel follows two rather enigmatic sayings related to the *basileia* (vv. 21–25).

Questions

1. Where have readers of Mark (up to 4:1–2) previously encountered the expression "kingdom/*basileia* of God"?
2. Where, in the first parable (4:26–29), do you think the emphasis should be put: on the sower, the process of growth, or the harvest? Why?
3. What distinguishes the second parable from the first and what does it add, if anything, to your understanding of the mystery of the *basileia*?

⊹ ❦ ❧ ⊹

4. How does the change of audiences in the various segments affect your interpretation of the entire parable discourse?
5. Why do you think commentators, translators, and even the lectionary, connect the second parable (vv. 30–32) with such passages as Ezekiel 17:23 and 31:6 (as well as Daniel 4:9.18)?
6. Do you think the tension between verses 33 and 34 (see also vv. 10–12) could be the key to understanding the whole discourse?

Interpretive points

1. *Why different audiences?* One interesting feature of the proposed con-
    centric or "chiastic" structure of the parable discourse (4:1–34) is
    worth noting. Jesus' instructions to "those who were around him
    along with the Twelve" (v. 10) are placed at the center of the discourse
    (D, but also C and C¹), while the three seed parables (B and B¹) are
    spoken to the crowds. This change of audiences may affect, signifi-
    cantly, one's interpretation not only of the whole passage, but also of
    the two seed parables (4:26–32) that make up today's lection.

2. *A master parable.* Although Jesus' teaching "many things in parables" to
    crowds of people by the lakeside (4:1–2) is presented as one particu-
    lar incident, the use of the Greek imperfect tense for "teaching"—
    here and in the concluding verses (33–34)—indicates otherwise.
    Designating habit or repetition—a difficult tense to render in Eng-
    lish—this Greek imperfect suggests that we are offered here a sum-
    mary of Jesus' teaching activity "in parables." Concurring with this,
    the parable of the Sower, and its allegorical interpretation, is better
    understood as a master parable in which the different fates of the seeds
    become images for different responses, negative and positive, to Jesus
    and his teaching throughout the Gospel (Donahue-Harrington, 147).

3. *More parables of the* basileia. For most Christians, and rightly so, parables are
    little stories with a message. From this perspective, the parables of Jesus as
    a genre are no different from those of the rabbis, or from modern and
    contemporary parables, or even from these little stories that many preach-
    ers use in their sermons or homilies. In all cases, the "story" intends to
    communicate something that, perhaps, only stories can tell, or tell better
    than any other means of communication. So what may distinguish Jesus'
    parabolic stories from other parables are not the parables themselves, but
    their content. In Mark 4, this content is the mystery of God's *basileia*.

Pastoral and homiletical notes

1. *Without context . . .* Of the important parable discourse in Mark 4, both
    lectionaries have only retained the last two small parables about the

basileia and its conclusion (vv. 33–34). As our interpretive points suggest, the thrust, as well as the function, of these parables and conclusion cannot be grasped outside of their narrative context (Mark 4).

2. *What about relevancy?* Some interpreters make a case for interpreting the last two parables as words of hope for a persecuted and discouraged community. Though most interesting, this historical reading begs important questions for today. What are we to make of this emphasis on God's future action at the expense of both the activity and comprehension of the human collectivity? How can, or do, these parables speak words of hope in our time? The extraordinary space allocated to the "failures" of the sowing may stand as testament to the struggles of the world in which we live, while the images of both the harvest and the greatest of all shrubs remain as a reminder of what the future may hold.

3. *Speaking of God's future in difficult contexts.* If the future belongs to God, and to God alone, what is one to make of these recent horrendous attempts to "force" the advent of the *basileia*, or of the escalating invasion by apocalyptic prophets on our TV screens, or again, of the frightening rise in the spread of Satanic cults? These and similar trends constitute part of the context—our contemporary context—in which these small parables are to be proclaimed in a way that makes them relevant. This may prove a colossal task for any preacher or communicator of the Word!

4. *Insiders and outsiders.* Both parables, as well as the warning issued in 4:24–25, should caution preachers against rushing to identify who the "insiders" and "outsiders" are. As we continue through Mark's Gospel, the sharp distinction between the two groups (vv. 10–12) will quickly become blurred. Outsiders may become insiders, and insiders, outsiders. No one escapes the paradox of the Gospel.

5. *Thinking theologically.* Both readings present a theological vision of God's involvement in the establishment of a renewed Davidic dynasty for Israel (Ezekiel) and of the kingdom/*basileia* of God (Mark). The challenge for preachers will be how to help congregations understand what their involvement should be in making this theological vision a reality.

18. Twelfth Sunday in Ordinary Time
Proper 7
Year B

Roman Catholic L	*Revised Common L*
Job 38:1, 8–11	Job 38:1–11
Mark 4:35–41	Mark 4:35–41

Overcoming the Forces of the Primeval Waters
(Mark 4:35–41)

On Job 38:1–11

At the heart of the book of Job is the human quest for the meaning of suffering in a world ruled by an almighty and sovereign God. The "righteous" Job rejects the conventional wisdom and theology espoused by his three friends and dares to question and challenge this God. The response of God starts in chapter 38, and contrary to expectation, takes the form of a series of questions that Job is asked to face "like a man" (38:3). Job's humble admission that he may have spoken too quickly about things that he did not understand (42:3) is not, however, the end of this debate. Job's friends are quickly admonished for not speaking of [God] correctly, "as my servant Job has" (42:7).

Today's selection constitutes the beginning of God's long, overpowering response to Job's accusations and challenge. The first questions set the tone for this entire response: Job was not there when God created the earth (vv. 4–7) or took control over the primeval waters (vv. 8–11). What does it mean to face a sovereign and overpowering God "like a man"? One thing is made very clear, that it is okay for humans to question God and God's actions! As in the time of Job, many of us, today, will find this view of God problematic.

On Mark 4:35–41
Context

This "mighty act" of Jesus, the first of a grouping of four, immediately follows Jesus' parabolic teaching (4:1–34) and begins the next subsection (4:35–5:43) of the second major division of Mark's Gospel (3:7–6:6a). In addition to the Muzzling of the Storm (4:35–41), this group includes the exorcism of the Gerasene Demoniac (5:1–20), and two intertwined stories, the healing of the Woman with a Flow of Blood and the raising of Jairus' Daughter (5:21–43).

In 4:1, Jesus was forced to get into a boat because of the crushing pressure of the large crowd surrounding him, and it is from the boat that he begins to teach the crowds (v. 2). When the teaching is finished, and evening descends, Jesus asks his disciples ("them") to cross the lake. This is the beginning of the first of two sea journeys in Mark's Gospel and it will take Jesus and his disciples back and forth across the lake (cf. 5:1, 21).

Questions

1. Where is the "other side" located, geographically and theologically, and whom are the people "taking Jesus with them in the boat" (v. 36)?
2. Why is Jesus said to "rebuke" the wind and "silence" (muzzle) the sea? Does Mark's use of these very same words in 1:25 have any effect on the meaning of this story?
3. Do you think that Jonah 1 may have influenced the construction of this miracle story?

⊬— ❦ ❦ —⊱

4. Why is Jesus addressed as "teacher" and where has this title originated in the previous chapters of Mark?
5. Where in Mark have you already encountered a Christological reaction similar to that of verse 41?
6. What is your primary understanding of "miracles" and in what way do you see this miracle story in relation to God's *basileia*?

Interpretive points

1. *Discerning the 'miracle.'* There are many ways one can read a miracle story, but for the sake of this discussion, let us consider two "basic" ap-

proaches. A literal reading would hold that things happened exactly as reported in Mark: Jesus, one day, calmed a storm on the lake that threatened the life of his disciples, revealing at the same time something of his divine power. Conversely, a narrative reading of the same story will focus, not on what Jesus may have done some two thousand years ago, but rather on what happens in the text. It will pay more attention to the context in which the story is located, details in the text that otherwise might not be attended to, and what Jesus and the other characters are doing in the text. After your analysis, do you think a literal or narrative reading best conveys what this story is about?

2. *Parabolic stories.* Miracles are like parables in that they also need to be interpreted. But unlike the parables in Mark, such interpretation is not given, at least not explicitly, to the disciples. Here, as elsewhere, they are having a hard time figuring out what is going on (see Mark 8:17–21). To be quite blunt, they just never seem to get it! Unlike the disciples, however, the readers are often given inside knowledge about Jesus (1:1–13). That is not the case here, and both the readers and disciples are kept in the dark. Just like parables, miracle stories are "metaphoric" and parabolic. To have their deeper meaning revealed, they require interpretation.

3. *Exorcizing the forces of evil.* Jesus' use of the verbs "rebuke" and "muzzle," often translated as "silence," is a rather unusual way to speak to a raging sea. He has used identical language earlier to free a man afflicted with an unclean spirit (1:23–26). Could this former use serve as an indication of how to interpret this present action of Jesus? Perhaps, Jesus needs to "exorcize" the powers of the sea because they are trying to prevent him and his disciples from reaching Gentile land on the other side of the lake, the country of the Gerasenes (5:1) and of the Decapolis (5:20). The implications of this interpretation are huge. Hermeneutically and pastorally, the story of "The Stilling of the Storm" takes on a whole new meaning.

4. *Using First Testament models.* This is not the only story in Mark to echo First Testament stories or motifs. Knowledge of Jonah 1 will help understand how the author makes use of these echoes or stories and

motifs to articulate the "high Christology" we find in this text of Mark. Familiarity with such First Testament stories will help us to hear the full message being conveyed in these texts.

Pastoral and homiletical notes

1. *The power of miracle stories.* Preaching miracle stories is no easy task. Whatever one's view of miracles is, no one, in my judgment, can dismiss the exegetical, hermeneutical, and pastoral issues such texts raise in the contexts of our day.

2. *A metaphorical reading.* What could the fears of the disciples found in this narrative convey to us about the challenges the community of Mark may have been facing? In this historical context, the fears could not refer to an "incident" in the life of Jesus' disciples, dated some forty years earlier. Something else was obviously worrying the community or its leaders. Another Markan story may be more explicit about what this fear or worry might have been (7:24–31).

3. *The journey to faith.* One needs faith to confess Jesus as the Christ, Son of God (1:1), and to understand what he is about. According to Jesus, this is a faith that the disciples are still missing at this point in the Gospel. This story provides a great opportunity to also make use of metaphors and to introduce the faith journey of the disciples as a model of the struggles and difficulties we encounter in our own faith journeys.

4. *Jesus, a miracle worker?* The question of the historicity of the miracles of Jesus should not be avoided, but discussed openly. One point that ought to be stressed in such discussion is the influence of the Jewish tradition, of the prophetic tradition in particular, upon the elaboration of several miracle stories. Awareness of such influence, while serving as an antidote to reading these stories as proof-texts of the divinity of Jesus, will help readers to focus on the important Christological message that these stories want to convey.

19. Thirteenth Sunday in Ordinary Time
Proper 8
Year B

Roman Catholic L
Wisdom 1:13–15; 2:23–24
Mark 5:21–43

Revised Common L
Wisdom 1:13–15; 2:23–24
Mark 5:21–43

FROM DEATH TO LIFE
(MARK 5:21–43)

ON WISDOM 1:13–15; 2:23–24

In this book presumably written in the first-century BCE, in Alexandria, a Jew is encouraging his fellow Jews to continue living proudly and faithfully in the midst of an ever threatening, and increasingly immoral, Hellenistic Culture. For this author, the only route to immortality is righteous living and he begins this book with a series of exhortations on how to live righteously. In order to respond more adequately to problems of his day and to help his people live through their present crisis, the author reinterprets past biblical traditions.

The first reading consists of two sections, the first section concluding the exhortation to be righteous and the second, concluding a diatribe against the "wicked." This text reminds us that humans are created for immortality and that the devil, not God, is responsible for the spiritual death of the wicked. Although connections can be seen to the first chapters of Genesis, the views expressed here go far beyond those espoused in the Hebrew bible.

ON MARK 5:21–43
Context

Jesus and the disciples have barely reached the other side of the lake, the country of the Gerasenes in Gentile territory (5:1–2), when he is immediately confronted by "a man out of the tomb with an unclean spirit," and challenged not to torment him (v. 7). A strange twist occurs in this bizarre episode when people from the neighboring cities, disturbed by what has happened to the herd of pigs and the possessed man, beg Jesus to leave their neighborhood (vv. 14–17). After this, his first entry into Gentile territory, Jesus returns by boat with his disciples to the west bank of the lake, back into Jewish territory. As usual, crowds quickly gather around him (5:21). Immediately following the entry of Jesus back into Jewish territory, we are presented with two intertwining stories that conclude a grouping of four of his "mighty works" (4:35—5:43). These stories, the raising of Jairus' daughter and the "salvation" of the hemorrhaging woman (5:21–43), make up our Gospel reading of today.

Questions

1. What do you think of the kind of faith the woman is displaying in her approach to Jesus? Find support for your answer in the text.
2. In light of the statement, "Daughter, your faith has made you well" (v. 34), what do you perceive Jesus' role to be in this healing?
3. Considering the sandwich technique employed by Mark, which one of these two stories do you think is intended to illuminate the other?

⊷ ❦ ❧ ⊶

4. Find elements, details, or words in both segments of the first story that may reflect life in post-resurrection communities?
5. Do you think the "purity code" from Leviticus 15 has anything to do with the story of the Woman with a Flow of Blood? If so, what?
6. Can you think of any connection between the fact that the girl was twelve years old and the woman had been bleeding for twelve years?

Interpretive points

1. *Women disciples.* One fourth of all the persons listed in Mark are women. Four out of these thirteen women play central narrative roles. In addition to the hemorrhaging woman, we find the Syrophoenician woman (7:24–31), the poor widow (12:41–44), and the anointing woman (14:3–8). These four women are not named, but are portrayed in a very positive light. In sharp contrast to the male disci-

ples who have difficulty understanding Jesus and his message, these women are presented as models of faith, of initiative and boldness, and of theological insight. In short, they are presented as examples of discipleship. While the rather bleak picture of the male disciples will serve its purpose down the road, readers and preachers should not lose sight of how Mark portrays these women.

2. *Bold faith.* Whatever their literary history, Mark joins these stories by using his sandwich technique, calling for both stories to be interpreted together, to throw light on each other. Faith is one of the central themes connecting the two episodes. For example, the bold faith of the hemorrhaging woman serves as an ideal that Jairus must strive for. While Jesus tells the woman, "*your* faith has made you well," he encourages Jairus, who has just witnessed the bold action of the woman, not to fear but only to believe. Readers cannot fail to compare the faith responses found in these two stories with the previous lack of faith found in the disciples on the lake (4:40) and in the upcoming lack of faith found in Jesus' hometown (6:6).

3. *From death to life.* The number twelve connects these two stories. In a society that defines women by their procreative capacity, the young woman is dead at the very age where she would be expected to give life, and the mature woman is dead, socially, because of her inability to bring forth life. Through faith, these women are restored to wholeness and integrated back into society.

Pastoral and homiletical notes

1. *Keep the text as is.* The important literary and thematic connections between the two stories play against omitting, as the shorter reading in the *Roman Catholic Lectionary* suggests, the story of the Hemorrhaging Woman.

2. *Boldly breaking taboos.* Jesus continues to break taboos, to overcome barriers. Here, he has no qualms about touching the girl's dead body or about being touched by a "ritually unclean" woman. Who, one may ask however, actually breaks the taboo or the barrier of ritual purity,

Jesus or the woman? In her bold attempt to reach for and touch Jesus' garments, it is the woman who breaks the barrier of the Torah prescription (Lev 15) despite the risks involved. Jesus does not reprimand the woman but agrees with her, affirming her faith.

3. *Touching Jesus' garment.* Taboos exist today, as they did at the time of Jesus, and some of these taboos, just like that woman's chronic bleeding, have societal and religious repercussions. The hemorrhaging woman's faith compelled her to craft her own reinsertion into community. We are left to wonder what will happen when the people we exclude from our communities craft their own way back based on the strength of their faith. We are also left to wonder what the Jesus of Mark's Gospel would have to say about the taboos we embrace that keep people on the outside of our faith communities. How, as community, are we going to react when they decide to touch "Jesus' garment"?

4. *A socio-political analysis.* Writing from a postcolonial perspective, Musa W. Dube, a woman scholar from Lesotho, has translated the story of the bleeding woman of Mark's Gospel into a story about her country, "Mama Africa." Africa has been bleeding for more than half a century at the hands of imperial and neo-colonial forces. Discovering that none of these powers-that-be have done her any good, Dube wonders if "Mama Africa," like the hemorrhaging woman, will finally turn to Jesus. Will Africa, like the hemorrhaging woman, take matters in her own hands with all the risks involved, trusting in Jesus' vision of the *basileia*?

20. Fourteenth Sunday in Ordinary Time
Proper 9
Year B

Roman Catholic L
Ezekiel 2:2–5
Mark 6:1–6

Revised Common L
Ezekiel 2:2–5
Mark 6:1–13

Rejection of the Prophet from Nazareth
(Mark 6:1–6)

On Ezekiel 2:2–5

As with many other prophetic books, the book of Ezekiel opens with an "account" of the prophet's vocation. This account, similar to the book of Hosea (1—3), covers almost three chapters (1—3:15/27). The story begins with the priest Ezekiel experiencing a majestic throne vision in which the glory of God on its way to Babylon is revealed (1:4–28). The call and commission of the prophet follows this vision (2—3:15). To equip Ezekiel for the difficult task of preaching God's words of judgment (3), he is instructed to "eat the scroll" on which are written "words of lamentation and mourning and woe" (2:10).

In today's reading, Ezekiel, a "mortal," is singled out to become a prophet of the exile. His mission will be to speak God's word of judgment to a "rebellious and stubborn people." Many will likely refuse to accept the words that God has instructed Ezekiel to pronounce (2:5).

On Mark 6:1–6
Context

The second major section of Mark's Gospel concludes, just like the first did (cf. 3:1–6), with the rejection of Jesus, here by his townsfolk and family members, there by the joined forces of the Pharisees and Herodians. These signs of opposition to Jesus and their location in the narrative are significant. They serve not only as a contrast to what could be interpreted as his successful journey around the lake, but also as an indication that not everyone is willing or able to understand the teachings of Jesus.

Today's episode follows two mighty acts performed by Jesus, after returning to the west bank of the lake, in Jewish Galilee. Leaving the lakeside, or the house of Jairus, Jesus and his disciples make the roughly forty-kilometer journey to his hometown of Nazareth (cf. 1:9, 24). The fact that the disciples are with him may alert the reader that what follows is no mere family visitation. Even if they play no further role in the story, their presence is an indication that this visit is part of Jesus' continuing mission and, consequently, also part of their training.

Questions

1. Does the information, given in verse 3, cause you discomfort or raise questions of faith for you?
2. What causes the townsfolk to move from astonishment (v. 2) to offense or scandal (v. 3)?
3. What issues are raised by this passage that may be of relevance to our churches of today?

↤ ❦ ❧ ↦

4. What makes scholars identify this story as a "pronouncement story"?
5. Can Jesus' statement in verse 4 be reconciled with what people will say of him in 6:15 and 8:28?
6. Is the narrator's comment that Jesus could not do any "miracle" there consistent with what you have already read in Mark?

Interpretive points

1. *Faith and miracles?* Mark offers different views on whether faith in Jesus is necessary for him to perform mighty deeds. The narrator's remark that Jesus could do no deed of power there stands in stark contrast to stories where faith allows Jesus to do deeds of power (1:21–28; 1:40–45 and 2:1–12). Does this mean that such deeds can only be understood, or even done, in the context of faith?

2. *Familiarity breeds contempt.* The reaction of Jesus' hometown to his wisdom and deeds of power is déjà vu. The scribes from Jerusalem questioned the origin of Jesus' power to exorcize demons (3:22, 30), and here people from his own town find it impossible to connect the wisdom of Jesus with the miraculous activity to God (6:2). At the surface level of the text, it is the familiarity of this "village boy" that causes the people of Nazareth and his own family to so negatively react to him. The townspeople and Jesus' family are akin to the "outsiders" who hear his parables but do not understand (4:11–12). Jesus' own explanation is that no one is a prophet in their own country (6:4). In other words, familiarity breeds contempt.

3. *Son of Mary?* What is one to make of the peculiar designation "son of Mary"? Two of the most prominent scholarly suggestions need mentioning. This description of Jesus owes either to the simple fact that Joseph had long been dead or that he came from a dubious or illegitimate origin. Whatever one makes of this second opinion, there is no ground for interpreting the expression "son of Mary" in reference to a virginal conception of Jesus.

4. *Beware of anti-Jewish propaganda.* Language of rejection is dangerous; perhaps more so in a religious book such as the Bible. It can easily be hijacked for religious-political causes, as too many recent and not-so-recent tragic events have fully demonstrated. Regrettably, the rejection of Jesus by his hometown and his own family could be and, in point of fact, has been used to symbolize his rejection by the Jewish people. Interpreting the story in this light transforms a story about an event in the life of Jesus into anti-Jewish propaganda.

Pastoral and homiletical notes

1. *A strange decision!* Today's Gospel selection from the *Revised Common Lectionary* includes, in addition to the incident in Nazareth, the Sending Out of the Twelve (6:6b–13). The incident in Nazareth ends the second major structural division of this Gospel and scholars generally do not associate the sending of the Twelve with it. The Sending/Commission of the Twelve, which is the Gospel reading for next

Sunday in the *Roman Catholic Lectionary*, will be discussed in the following chapter.

2. *A powerless Jesus!* For the first time in Mark, Jesus is shown to have limitations. Human resistance or lack of faith makes him powerless. Nothing to this point appeared to limit his power to proclaim the *basileia* in both words and mighty deeds. It will become clear in the second half of the Gospel that the Jesus of Mark, despite appearances, is no mere miracle worker. He appears to be particularly concerned with people's appetite for such power displays. In describing the powerlessness of Jesus, this episode in Nazareth subverts this power game and prepares for the great paradox of the cross. What an occasion to address the paradox we often perceive in our own lives concerning the power of God!

3. *His own family among the "outsiders"!* The rejection of Jesus by his own family recalls the curious incident of 3:21 where his relatives try to get hold of their sibling, thinking he is out of his mind. Like many of Jesus' townsfolk, they are unable to "hear" and "see" what his wisdom and deeds of power speaks of him. They too stand among the "outsiders."

4. *Faith cannot be taken for granted.* Where faith already exists, it must be nurtured and cared for as a treasure, for it can be eroded, undermined, or even lost. There are many things that can cause people to abandon their faith and trust in Jesus or to leave their faith community. As communities of faith we are called to provide an open and welcoming environment that nurtures each person's faith journey. Communities that find it difficult to accept diversity in faith values may run the risk of leaving persons as Jesus was left, feeling rejected and powerless.

5. *Just like Ezekiel?* The connection between the first reading and the Gospel is rather obvious. Both Ezekiel and Jesus are prophets whose "words and deeds" are not accepted by their own people.

21A. FIFTEENTH SUNDAY IN ORDINARY TIME
Year B

Roman Catholic L
Amos 7:12–15
Mark 6:7–13

THE COMMISSION OF THE TWELVE
(MARK 6:7–13)

ON AMOS 7:12–15

Although the book of Amos provides no direct account of the prophet's call, the confrontation between the priest Amaziah and Amos is regarded as fulfilling this role. Contrary to expectations, it is located in the third and last major section of the book (7:10–17), interrupting a series of five visions of Amos regarding Israel's coming judgment and destruction (7—9:10). In its present location in the book, this confrontation between priest and "prophet" serves to legitimate Amos' message of inescapable destruction that God has compelled him to prophesy.

In the first two visions, Amos intercedes and God relents. In the last three, God does not relent and the fate of the Northern kingdom of Israel is sealed. The king and his spokesperson, priest Amaziah, refuse to accept God's judgment. At stake, in the power game that follows is the issue of jurisdiction. Who has the authority to determine who speaks for Israel—the king or God? In the last three visions of Amos, God provides the answer.

ON MARK 6:7–13
Context

For the great majority of commentators, the third section of the Gospel of Mark begins, like the first two, with a commissioning story of disciples (1:16–20 and 3:13–19). The end of this section is disputed. Some maintain that it ends in 8:21 while others include the climatic confession of Peter in Caesarea in 8:27–30.

After being rejected by his hometown, Jesus sends the Twelve "two by two" on their first and only mission—with authority over the unclean spirits. Readers of Mark already know of Jesus' design concerning the ones he has chosen. To the first four called to follow, he has said: "I will make you fishers of men [people]" (1:17). Later, Jesus speaks of the Twelve he has chosen as the ones "to be with him, and to be sent out to proclaim the message, and to have authority to cast out demons" (3:14–15). These disciples have now "been with Jesus" for a while, hearing his teaching and watching him perform mighty deeds. They are now ready—so apparently thinks their teacher!—to go out and do the same kind of work that they have observed Jesus doing. Their mission will conclude with their return, enthusiastically reporting to Jesus in 6:30.

Questions

1. Why do you think Jesus gives the Twelve the particular instructions for the road that he gives? Do you see any relevance for our world today?
2. Jesus instructs the disciples to "shake the dust off their feet" if they find themselves rejected in a town. Does this reflect Jesus' own attitude that we find throughout this Gospel?

✦ ❦ ❦ ✦

3. Can you think of textual or historical reasons that would explain Jesus' decision to send the Twelve "two by two"?
4. Is there anywhere in this passage that you think the author may be providing a window into an early Church context or situation?
5. Why do you think Mark has sandwiched the story of the murder of John the Baptist (6:14–29) between the mission of the Twelve (7:6b–13) and their return in verse 30?

Interpretive points

1. *Cynic connection?* One solid conclusion of the biblical method known as Redaction criticism is that the Gospels were all written to and for spe-

cific Christian communities. Sometimes, as in this case, the only way to make sense of certain passages from the Gospels rests on our capacity to link such texts to their most likely historical contexts. For example, in their quest for meaning, a number of scholars suggest that the prescriptions of verses 8–9 are a response—from Jesus or the early Church—to the Cynic ("wandering") philosophers from whose lifestyle they sought to differentiate themselves. Unlike their Cynic counterparts, Jesus' disciples are instructed to take for their journey no bread or provision bag, and only one tunic (that is, the clothes on their backs!), but, like the Cynics, they can wear sandals. Raising this complex historical issue brings another dimension to our reading. If we find that these strange prescriptions were a response to the lifestyle of the Cynics, we have to wonder of what relevance they are to the evangelizers of today.

2. *Ascetism or insecurity?* Connected to the previous discussion is the suggestion by some that there is an ascetic touch to those prescriptions that actually reflect Jesus' own attitude and behavior, as he travels through the villages and cities of Upper Galilee. Readers may be hard pressed to find anything in Mark to warrant such a conclusion. A more promising route might be to see these prescriptions as a warning against the temptation to look for too much security in the missionary task ahead.

3. *Whose mission?* A more interesting question would be to ask why a mission at all? The reader may be struck by how quickly it ends, with barely one verse allotted for its outcome (v. 30). The unique portrayal of the disciples in Mark's Gospel makes this mission "impossible"— not in historical, but in rhetorical terms. Although they have attended the school of Jesus, been "with him" for a while, listened to his teaching, and witnessed his mighty acts, they have learned little. As a matter of fact, concerning their understanding of the miracles of the loaves, both the narrator (6:51–52) and Jesus himself (8:17–21) say they have learned nothing. Why then, one may ask, would Jesus involve them in his task or mission? Perhaps, these instructions, written after the death and resurrection of Jesus, are addressed, not to the disciples of Jesus, but to those early communities already involved in the task of evangelizing.

Pastoral and homiletical notes

1. *Rejection is the link.* Preachers using the *Revised Common Lectionary* selection for last Sunday (6:1–13) may find themselves hard pressed to choose between the rejection of Jesus in his hometown and the sending out of the Twelve. Yet, the second episode also evokes the possibility of rejection—the central theme in the Nazareth incident.

2. *A missionary Church.* In their recent commentary of Mark, both Donahue and Harrington view the instructions given by Jesus in this passage (6, 7–13) as part of the missionary origin of the Church (*Mark*, 194). As suggested earlier, these instructions may serve as a warning to the disciples not to expect missionary work and security to go hand in hand. Missionary work always involves risk. The reading, today, may provide the opportunity for our Christian communities to reflect on what they are willing to risk as part of the task or mission of Jesus.

3. *Unprepared, but willing.* An obvious connection exists between our first reading, the call and commissioning of an unprepared Amos (I was no prophet), and the Gospel reading of the unprepared disciples. Both Amos and the disciples are called to stand for justice and peace. In their world as in ours, this task is impossible without some measure of personal insecurity and risk.

4. *Teaching biblical methods.* This passage may provide an excellent occasion for initiating congregations to the various layers of Gospel texts. Texts such as this were written within a community of believers to address issues that arose as people sought to live out their faith in the risen Christ. Jesus speaks to us in many ways through the Gospels. Perhaps, here as in other places, he is speaking through the early community to inform and encourage other communities. Are the issues this community is facing so different from the issues of our faith communities of today?

Revised Common L
Amos 7:7–15
Mark 6:14–29

Flashback on the Murder of John the Baptist
(Mark 6:14–29)

On Amos 7:7–15

For the study guide on Amos 7:7–15, see chapter 21a.

On Mark 6:14–29
Context

The episode of the execution of John the Baptist (6:14–29) interrupts the flow of the narrative. Set between the account of the Sending out of the Twelve (6:6b–13) and their return (6:30), it provides an interlude for the disciples to go out on their mission and return to Jesus. This is another example of the now familiar sandwich technique of the evangelist.

The story of the Baptist's murder, limited to 6:17–29, is introduced by a brief discussion about rumors concerning Jesus—prompting King Herod and people to wonder about his true identity (6:14–16). This introduction is important for two reasons. First, it introduces the story that follows as an explanation of this brief discussion about Jesus (see "for" = Greek *gar*) and, second, it connects Jesus with the only Gospel story not about him. The significance of this last comment will not be lost on the reader.

Questions

1. What role do you think verses 14–16 play in the interpretation of the whole story?
2. According to Mark's Gospel, who is responsible for the death of John the Baptist?
3. Why do you think so many interpreters and artists have focused on Herodias and her daughter rather than on King Herod?

4. How does this text describe the characters and actions of Herod, Herodias, and her daughter?
5. Why do you think the evangelist chose to insert this episode between the Sending out of the Twelve and their return to Jesus? Has the evangelist Matthew preserved this arrangement?
6. Compare Mark's story of John's execution with the Jewish historian Josephus' version of it in *Antiquities* 18:116–119. What do you make of the differences in both accounts?

Interpretive points

1. *A double narrative function.* Besides addressing the question of the historical reliability of Mark's version of the story—as compared to the account of Josephus—interpreters have focused on the purpose or function of this episode in Mark's narrative. Two functions of this "flashback" on the Baptist' death are of particular interest. The first concerns Jesus. Presented as the forerunner of Jesus' message and ministry at the beginning of the Gospel narrative (1:2–8), John the Baptist is now introduced as the forerunner of his death, the plan for which is already in motion (3:6). A second function regards the disciples. Sandwiched between the stories of the mission of the Twelve, this murder story may also point to the mortal danger faced by evangelizers, in fact, by any disciple of Jesus.

2. *Feminist critique of male voyeurism.* Over the centuries, this episode has generated a variety of readings and interpretations in literature, paintings, music, and movies. As one of the Gospel stories most frequently portrayed in Christian art and other artistic forms (Bach), it has left

its mark on peoples' imagination. Many readers may not be surprised that the main focus of these readings and representations has been, unmistakably, on the "dancing girl." As Girard states, "the dancer and her dance have always fired the erotic and aesthetic imagination of the West" (p. 311). Using gender as an analytic tool, feminist critics have raised the specter of male construction of women as objects "to be looked at." The active voyeurism or lust of Herod and his guests in both the Gospel story and its various artistic representations would appear to support this construction. One disturbing consequence of this male construction is that it supports the notion that women are in some way responsible for the lust of men who gaze at them. Some critics go further and contend that many Christian interpreters of this biblical story have followed the trend, also highlighting the actions and activities of the women instead of fixing their gaze directly on Herod. Although Herod takes full responsibility for the execution of the prophet (6:16), many attribute that responsibility to Herodias, not to mention her daughter. In this light, the story is used "to blame female behavior for male lust and thus to legitimate association of women with sexuality and evil" (Dewey, *Mark*, 483).

Pastoral and homiletical notes

1. *Unexplained omission.* For unknown reasons, the episode of the Baptist's martyrdom was omitted from the *Roman Catholic Sunday Lectionary.* The story, without the important verses introducing the episode (vv. 14–16), is used for the feast of the Beheading of St. John the Baptist, celebrated on August 29.

2. *Male voyeurism in our Scriptures.* Given the way this story has been read and interpreted in literature and arts over the centuries, preachers face an obvious challenge. However it may provide a welcome opportunity to address the issue of how biblical texts have been, and can be, used to support the construction of women as objects. There may be multiple reasons for this, but in this story it appears to be male voyeurism.

3. *A daring message!* Congregations should also be helped to discover the purpose of this narrative in the context of Mark's Gospel. As indi-

cated, it is clearly not the purpose of the passage to tell readers how John the Baptist actually died, but rather that he was killed because of his daring prophetic activity. Having this story sandwiched between the Sending out of the Twelve and their return, it also tells readers that Jesus, the disciples, or any followers of Jesus, may end up suffering a similar fate. Whoever threatens the System will pay a price. John the Baptist did. Amos did. At the end of Mark's Gospel, Jesus also will. Any followers of Jesus whose proclamation is unacceptable to the powers that be also face the possibility of a similar fate.

Year B

Roman Catholic L	*Revised Common L*
Jeremiah 23:1–6	Jeremiah 23:1–6
Mark 6:30–34	Mark 6:30–34, 53–56

Like Sheep without a Shepherd
(Mark 6:30–34)

On Jeremiah 23:1–6

The first half of the book of Jeremiah contains oracles of judgment against Judah and Jerusalem (2—25:13). In today's passage, the prophet concludes his indictments of the last kings of Judah during the turbulent period leading to the Babylonian exile (21:11—23:8). The author does not explicitly mention the last of these kings, Zedekiah, but uses the meaning of his name (the LORD is righteousness) to proclaim the restoration of the Davidic dynasty through Zedekiah's reign.

In the first part of the passage a judgment oracle against the bad "shepherds" of Israel who have failed the people (23:1–2) is juxtaposed with God's promise to bring back the people from their exile and rise up true shepherds to take care of them (vv. 3–4). With a more eschatological tone, the next two verses (5–6) switch to the vision of a future Davidic king who, through his wisdom, justice, and righteousness, will bring salvation to God's people, both Judah and Israel. Not surprisingly, this future king will bear the name of "The LORD is our righteousness."

ON MARK 6:30–34 (53–56)
Context

Today's reading begins with the return of the "apostles" from their successful mission journey (v. 30). Using his sandwich technique, Mark inserts the flashback of the murder of John the Baptist (6:14–29) to separate the sending out of the Twelve (vv. 6b–13) from their return (v. 30). He now resumes the thread of his narrative with a brief description of the return of the apostles and a failed attempt by Jesus to get them away from the crowd.

Questions

1. What do you make of Jesus' reaction to his disciples' report on their mission and why do you think he is inviting them to take some rest?
2. Taking into account the stories of Jesus' rejection in Nazareth (6:1–6a) and the murder of John the Baptist (6:16–29), what do you think of the disciples' enthusiasm over their "successful mission"?
3. What motivates Jesus' compassion, here and in 8:1–9?

↦ ❋ ❊ ↤

4. Why are the Twelve suddenly called "apostles" in verse 30?
5. How might other First Testament texts echoing the words "like sheep without a shepherd" help us to understand this passage?
6. Do you think Jesus' observation about how the lack of shepherds in Israel should be handled hold any relevance for our Churches today?

Interpretive points

1. *What have the Twelve learned?* Why does Jesus feel the returning "apostles" need a little rest in the wilderness? Perhaps they are stressed, overworked, and need some time away from the crowds that keep pressing them. Yet, one feels there is more to it. Readers of Mark will recall that following a long day in Capernaum Jesus got up very early the next morning and withdrew to a deserted place to pray. He wasn't there long when his own disciples hunted him down and reminded him that everyone was searching for him (1:35–39). Jesus then moved on bringing his message to the neighboring towns. In

the reading of today, however, whatever plan there was for a time of rest needs to be reassessed in light of this new situation. Following the disciples' fruitful mission, many people "from all the towns" now recognize both them and Jesus. The need for a time of rest is forgotten. Immediately upon seeing an "aimless and wandering" people, deprived of leadership, Jesus feels compassion for them and begins to "teach them many things" (v. 34). What happens to the disciples, one may ask? Unlike Jesus after his long day in Capernaum, the disciples fail to realize the demanding nature of their mission. Later, at sunset, they even urge Jesus to send the people away so that they can look after themselves. Jesus not only refrains from sending the people away but also informs the disciples that *they* themselves must feed them!

2. *Mark's important bread section.* The mission of the Twelve and their return introduce a cycle of seemingly parallel feeding stories (6:35–44 and 8:1–9), boat trips (6:45–56 and 8:10), controversies with Pharisees (7:1–23 and 8:11–13), more bread stories (7:24–31 and 8:14–21), and healing acts (7:32–37 and 8:22–26). However one organizes these chapters, I would suggest that the main focus of this third section of Mark's Gospel is on the "bread" that Jesus provides for all, Jews and non-Jews alike. As becomes clearer from a close reading of these chapters, this bread is to be understood as a metaphor for the revelation or salvation brought about by Jesus.

Unfortunately, the greater part of this crucial section of Mark is left out of the lectionary in order to make room for the entire chapter 6 of John on the Bread of Life. These omissions deprive Christians of two significant points made in these chapters. First, the important issue of the disciples' misunderstanding about the loaves (6:52 and 8:14–21) goes unnoticed. Second, as a result of the exclusion of both feeding stories and of Jesus' crucial conversation with the woman from Syrophoenicia, we miss an opportunity to meet a Jesus who is open enough to listen to and share with Jews and non-Jews alike. Preachers will do well to remember this specific context when the lectionaries return to Mark 7:1–23, 24–30, and 31–37, following the reading of John 6.

Pastoral and homiletical notes

1. *What a loss!* Whether on this or the following Sunday, preachers owe their congregation some explanation about the lectionaries' switch to John 6 for the upcoming few weeks. Then, when Mark is resumed, an introduction to Mark 6:30—8:21, including the omitted stories, would serve to contextualize our readings.

2. *More than meets the eye?* Some might say that the instances where Jesus invites his disciples to take a rest are too few to miss. Passages such as this may be interpreted as an invitation for stressed and overworked ministers to examine their own need for rest. Whether this is what lies behind Jesus' invitation is not immediately clear, but the pursuit of the crowd certainly plays havoc with his program. As we noted, readers, if not the apostles, might be told something else altogether. The focus of this story may not be on rest but, rather, on the demanding nature of the disciples' mission.

3. *Switches to John 6?* No one can dismiss the importance of John's chapter on the Bread of Life and one can certainly understand the Churches' desire to have their members exposed to the rich Johannine presentation. To allot five consecutive Sundays to almost the whole chapter tells of the importance attached to it. John has traditionally been interpreted in light of its Christological or/and Eucharistic content and is still being read so by many today. Is that how the chapter should be read? Preachers should be made aware of a lack of consensus among scholars on this matter. Whether this chapter should be read in Christological or Eucharistic terms, totally, only in part, or not at all, is still a wide open question.

4. *Jesus, the shepherd.* The *Revised Common Lectionary's* addition to the lection for today, of the summary of Jesus' healings in Gennesaret (Mark 6:53–56) can be seen as one more illustration, after the feeding story, of Jesus' shepherding role.

23. Twenty-Second Sunday in Ordinary Time
Proper 17
Year B

Roman Catholic L
Deuteronomy 4:1–2, 6–8
Mark 7:1–8, 14–15, 21–23

Revised Common L
Deuteronomy 4:1–2, 6–9
Mark 7:1–8, 14–15, 21–23

Pitting Torah against Torah?
(Mark 7:1–23)

On Deuteronomy 4:1–2, 6–8

The book of Deuteronomy is a long exhortation from Moses to the people of Israel, as they are about to enter the Promised Land. To live prosperously in the land, they will need to hear and observe "the statutes and ordinances" given them by Moses. The first reading of today marks the beginning of this central exhortation, which is preceded by one of the many reminders of what God has accomplished for them and their frequent insubordination. Today's selection is only the hortatory part—what Israel is required to do, not God's past saving actions for the people (flagged in v. 9 and described in vv. 10–14). It needs to be set in the context of God's mighty acts in Egypt and the Covenant at Mount Horeb. Such a theological foundation is crucial for a correct understanding of these "statutes and ordinances."

On Mark 7:1–23
Context

Mark 7:1–23 falls half way through what we have identified as the third major section of this Gospel (6:7—8:22/26). It is preceded by the stories of the first feeding (vv. 30–44) and Jesus walking on the water, ending on a rather surprising note concerning the disciples' misunderstanding of the "miracle" on account of their hardened hearts (v. 52). Interestingly, this discussion with Pharisees and scribes over issues of ritual purity will be followed by a number of parallel stories—all located this time in *Gentile* land (7:24—8:13).

Questions

1. Use the change of audiences to determine the major sections or divisions of this passage and identify what you think are the most important statements Jesus makes in each section.
2. What do you think of Jesus' use of the Isaiah passage to condemn the Pharisees' practice? Do you see this "contemporizing" or actualizing of Scripture as potentially dangerous?
3. In verses 14–15, does Jesus merely reject purity laws or is he abrogating parts of the Torah itself?
4. What do you think this section of Mark 7, if going unchallenged, can communicate to Christians of today about Jewish contemporary observance of their food laws?

↦ ❧ ❦ ↤

5. Do you think that Jesus' use of Scripture to reject certain religious rituals and practices as purely "human traditions" provide a hermeneutical tool for a critique of certain Christian rituals and practices of today?
6. Historical question: If Jesus had been that clear about rejecting all food laws (v. 19), why do you think it took so long for the early Church to deal with this issue (Gal 2:11–14 and Acts 10)?
7. In contrast with the "boundary markers" defining Judaism (circumcision, Sabbath, and food laws), what would you say are the "boundary markers" of Jesus' own group?

Interpretive points

1. *Different issues.* There is movement in this chapter. The discussion begins with a query over the failure of "some" of Jesus' disciples to ritually wash their hands before eating—leading Jesus to first denounce then illustrate the authority given to human traditions (traditions of the elders) over the Word of God. In verse 14, Jesus widens the dis-

cussion, raising the more fundamental issue of what defiles a person (v. 15) and going on to pronounce all foods clean (v. 19b). After declaring that "[only] the things that come out [of a person] are what defiles" (v. 15), he then catalogues behaviors and attitudes that defile a person (vv. 20–23).

2. *Is Jesus abrogating the Torah?* The practice of hand washing before eating was a tradition not shared by all, not even by all Pharisees, and so could be subject to criticism by Jesus. The dietary or kosher regulations (Lev 11—15; also Deut 14) were, however, a different matter. As part of the purity laws inscribed in the book of Leviticus, they could not be rejected without infringing upon the integrity of the Torah. Did Jesus declare all foods clean, as specified in 19b? One reason in particular would seem to militate against such a conclusion. Had Jesus been so clear about the issue of food laws, why was there so much acrimony over this problem in the early Church? Why did Peter have to be convinced by revelation to eat "unclean foods" (Acts 10) or challenged by Paul to eat with Gentile converts in Antioch (Gal 2)? This would explain a tendency among scholars to attribute such rejection not to Jesus but to the work of Mark, in response to, or as reflection of, what was emerging in his Christian community.

3. *A maverick Jesus.* This argument, cogent as it is, ought to be balanced by what is known of Jesus' generally free-lancing attitude towards some other purity laws—some of which mentioned in Leviticus 11—15. Touching a leper (1:41) or a corpse (5:41) would have made Jesus "unclean" in regard to the Law. His conviviality with "unclean" people like "sinners and tax collectors" is also well known. Whatever answer is given to this puzzle, the question remains, Why would Jesus, a Jew and always a Jew, reject the food laws?

4. *Ethical demands over purity laws, but . . .* Jesus' pronouncements in verses 15 and 21 may hold the key to this question. It is not what a person eats that defile, but "evil intentions" that come from within, from a person's heart (v. 21). What Jesus seems to be doing here is to place the primacy of ethical demands over purity laws and rituals—just as the prophets did. Rituals are subordinated to justice and love. If the

message is clear, the portrait it gives of the Pharisees and scribes is ambiguous, if not outright dangerous in our day and age. Are these "bad boys" of the Gospels to be understood as merely concerned with external matters such as food laws, paying little attention, if any, to what really defiles a person? Asking the question can be salutary for Christians whose heritage on this issue might still be compelling.

Pastoral and homiletical notes

1. *Supplying the missing context.* After 5 Sundays devoted to the reading of John 6, both lectionaries return with the first half of Mark 7 (vv. 1–23) to the semi-continuous reading of Mark's Gospel. As already noted, because of the omission of the two feeding stories, the notes concerning the disciples' misunderstanding about the loaves and, in the case of the *Roman Catholic Lectionary*, the crucial talk of Jesus with the Syrophoenician woman, Christians are deprived, not only of the narrative setting of Mark 7, but also of the role of this chapter in this section of Mark's Gospel. Preachers would do well to tell their congregations how Mark 7 acts like an "overture" to the Gentile mission—a "narrative hinge between the Jewish and Gentile phases of Jesus' ministry in the North sector" (France, 277).

2. *Wrestling with anti-Jewish perceptions.* The lectionary combination of Mark 7 and the text from Deuteronomy calls for some caution from preachers. If not handled with care, Jesus' harsh critique of the way the Pharisees and some scribes hold to human traditions over against God's commandments could easily transform Moses' exhortation to hear and obey the Torah into an indictment of the whole people of Israel.

3. *Respecting the identity of our Jewish sisters and brothers.* Jesus' rejection of the dietary laws should not lead to their trivializing. They certainly are not trivial practices for Jews. It should be remembered and also made clear that together with the practice of circumcision and the observance of Sabbath, dietary laws have always been "identity markers" for the Jewish people, today as yesterday. How would Christians react if "markers" of their own identity were threatened or dismissed? Is there a way to speak of defiling issues without denigrating an impor-

tant identity marker for Jews of all times? Aware of two thousand years of anti-Jewish sentiments, Christian preachers will remember that this text can still have the potential of perpetuating anti-Jewish contempt.

4. *What about our own rituals?* Traditions and ritual practices are the lot of all religions, including Christian denominations. Today's Gospel may be a welcome opportunity to reflect on the way we have come to use such traditions and practices in our own Churches.

24A. TWENTY-THIRD SUNDAY IN ORDINARY TIME
Year B

Roman Catholic L
Isaiah 35:4–7a
Mark 7:31–37

THE DEAF HEAR AND THE MUTE SPEAK
(MARK 7:31–37)

ON ISAIAH 35:4–7A

These verses, which befit a post-exilic situation, are part of a prophetic oracle of salvation. They come on the heels of a harsh judgment oracle against the nations, the neighboring Edom in particular (Chapter 34). The oracle of salvation is addressed to the dispersed people of Israel. It is a call to return to Zion through a desert (a flattened Edom?) transformed into a well-watered land (vv. 1 and 7). For the returning Israelites, God's vengeance (v. 4) will now take the forms of healing and hope for all that is amiss, restoration of sight and hearing, of walking and speech (vv. 5–6).

ON MARK 7:31–37
Context:

With Jesus moving even deeper into Gentile territory, the significance of the outcome of his encounter with the Syrophoenician woman can hardly be ignored. From the region of Tyre, his journey takes him further north to Sidon, then back south towards the Sea of Galilee, ending up on the east side of the lake in the Gentile district of the Decapolis—a region already visited in 5:1–20. There he is called upon to heal a deaf person with a serious speech impediment and a little later to feed another crowd of people, 4000 this time, before returning to the Jewish (western) shore of the lake.

Questions

1. How does the narrative context impact upon the meaning or significance of this story?
2. Why does Jesus look up to heaven, "groaning" or "sighing"? Where has he done this before in this Gospel?
3. What do you think this miracle story has to do with Jesus' mission to the Gentiles?

⊷ ❦ ❧ ⊶

4. "They beg him to lay his hand on him." What does Jesus do instead and what do you make of his rather elaborate healing technique?
5. Why do you think Jesus commands people to keep silent about this incident in Gentile territory, especially after giving some very different instructions to the demoniac from Gerasa (5:19)?

Interpretive points

1. *Narrative context.* In all our bibles (and commentaries), verse 31 introduces the healing of the deaf and mute man in the Decapolis region. Referring to the rather startling detour of Jesus into the Southern Phoenicia region, most commentators register their surprise at this odd geographical reference. Very few, too few in my estimation, raise the possibility that this information has a theological rather than merely geographical function. Structurally, the introduction to this healing story (v. 31) fits as well if not better as the conclusion to the Syrophoenician woman story. Either way, verse 31 forms the immediate context for both this last story and the subsequent feeding story (8:1–10). This context, I believe, preachers need to consider if they are to do justice to this text.

2. *Miracles are like parables.* Mark is fond of miracle stories. Miracle stories of one kind or another takes up a sizable portion of his Gospel, particularly in chapters 4 to 8. After 8:27, miracles will diminish considerably in the second half of this Gospel with a shift in focus to the suffering Messiah. Yet, it may be going too far to contrast too rigidly the "powerful Messiah" of the first eight chapters with the "suffering Messiah." Transforming the Jesus of the first half of the Gospel into a

"miracle worker" does not do justice to the profound theological teachings embedded in many of these stories. As we have already seen, there is more, much more, to these "miracle stories" than simply wonders performed by Jesus.

Let us now consider a parabolic reading of miracle stories. In a way, and this is certainly true of Mark's presentation, miracles are like parables. They need interpretation. Without explanation they will end up being no more than extraordinary occurrences. Unlike the parables, however, that are often explained in private to the disciples, miracles in Mark are nowhere further explained. Such explanation, embedded in these stories, is left for the reader to decipher. This is easier with some stories than with others. For example, the rather peculiar exchange between Jesus and the Syrophoenician woman helps readers to enter the parabolic dimension of the story. It moves them away from the immediate narrative setting into the larger context of the story, the issue of the mission to the Gentiles. Conversely, in the story of the deaf person with a serious speech impediment, the parabolic dimension is not immediately apparent. It needs to be construed, so to speak, out of the context in which the story is located. Attention to the people's reaction (v. 37) may indicate that there is more to this story than a miraculous healing of a person. A deaf person hears and a mute speaks. Gentile people hear and speak, for the first time publicly acknowledging Jesus as God's Messiah.

3. *Where are the disciples?* Their absence in both stories, Jesus' encounter with the Syrophoenician Woman and his healing of the Deaf Mute Man, is somewhat startling. If both stories indeed address the Gentile issue, the disciples would have gained an understanding by being there. Yet, they have not understood the miracle of the loaves (6:52), nor have they grasped the implications of Jesus' pronouncement and parable in 7:15–17. They are back with Jesus in the second feeding story, but according to Jesus' own words in 8:17–21, they don't fare any better. They do not understand about the loaves. They have yet to understand the true nature of the *basileia* that Jesus proclaims.

Pastoral and homiletical notes

1. *To be read in context.* In lectionaries, Gospel passages appear most of the time without their narrative context. Unless this context is introduced, before or after the reading in the homily, on this Sunday Christians will hear someone proclaim only the story of an extraordinary feat accomplished by Jesus. Also, without the Gentile context, preachers themselves will be hard pressed on this Sunday to move beyond the extraordinary feat to what transpires in the people's confession at the end of the story. As your own analysis may have shown, there is more to this passage than a simple miracle story. Christians should be afforded the opportunity to reflect upon what God may be telling them today through this story, read in both its narrative and contemporary context.

2. *Christological rereading.* "Absolutely overwhelmed" by what they have just witnessed, the people in the narrative recall the words of the prophet Isaiah and see their fulfillment in Jesus: "Then . . . the ears of the deaf [shall be] unstopped . . . and the tongue of the speechless sing for joy" (Isa 35:5–6). Although we are not told explicitly whether their utter astonishment transforms into Christian faith, their Christological rereading of the Isaiah text points in that direction. For these Gentiles, Jesus is now the Messiah, offering salvation to all, Jews and Gentiles alike. There is indeed more to this text than a simple miracle story.

3. *Healing as salvation?* In selecting the prophet Isaiah's vision of salvation for the first reading of today, the lectionary appears to be trying to stitch together Isaiah's promise of salvation with the healing activity of Jesus: of the Syrophoenician woman's daughter (7:24–30) and the deaf mute (7:31–37).

24b. Proper 18

Year B

Revised Common L
Proverbs 22:1–2, 8–9, 22–23

Mark 7:24–31

Learning from a Gentile Woman
(Mark 7:24–31)

On Proverbs 22:1–2, 8–9, 22–23

Attributed to the wise Solomon, these verses selected from Proverbs 22 speak to the interconnection between the wealthy and the poor, with a clear sympathy for the latter. Reputation and kindness are preferable to great wealth (22:1). Rich and poor may be part of creation (v. 2), but they are mutually bound to each other. The traditional vision that wicked people would be punished and righteous ones blessed in this world (vv. 8–9) was questioned in the books of Job and Ecclesiastes which both showed the limitations of such a theological view. This fact, however, should not be a license for injuring the poor and crushing the afflicted (22). Their plight is in the hands of a mighty counselor—the Lord "who pleads their cause" (23).

On Mark 7:24–31
Context

(For comments on 7:31–37, see previous chapter 24a.) The story of Jesus' encounter with a woman from the region of Tyre follows immediately the long debate about purity concerns (7:1–23). After what was said earlier about that debate, readers should have no difficulty in seeing the Gentile connection to this story.

Immediately following this story comes the information about Jesus' return to the sea of Galilee by a rather surprising geographical route through Sidon—to the north of Tyre! From there, Jesus turns southward, southeast of the lake, to the region of the Decapolis (ten cities)—by all accounts *Gentile* territory—where he will heal a deaf person, then proceed to feed 4000 people. Together with his disciples, he will then cross over to the western side of the lake, back into *Jewish* territory. The implications of Jesus' encounter with the Gentile woman will not be lost on the reader.

Questions

1. Note your initial reaction (or feelings) to this story. What would you say is most startling in the story?
2. What do you think is the difference, if any, between Jesus' view and that of the woman?
3. What do you think the story is really about? What is at issue and how is this issue (or problem) resolved? Why do you think the role of the problem solver is attributed to a woman?

✢ ✤ ✣ ✢

4. Is Jesus' statement in 7:27 not at odds with what he has said or implied earlier in Mark 7:14–23?
5. What is, in your view, the narrative role or function of the story in the overall structure of Mark 6:7—8:26?
6. Why do you think this story was included in Mark's Gospel? Can you think of a situation in his community that might have led the evangelist to insert that story in his Gospel?
7. Do you see any reason for including verse 31 in the story? After drawing out Jesus' circuit on a map, what do you make of Mark's geography?
8. What lesson do you think can be learned from this story about the need to listen to "victims" (underdogs) of political, social, and religious institutions?

Interpretive points

1. *A disquieting response from Jesus.* Jesus' strange response to the woman from Syrophoenicia (v. 27) has been and still today continues to be an

issue much debated among scholars. Harsh, rude, abusive, insulting, flippant, even cruel are only a sample of the epithets used in the literature to describe these words that strike us as so out of character for the Jesus we believe in. Christians are not accustomed to such a reaction from Jesus, especially toward a person seeking his help. The Jesus of the Gospels may not always be tender with some of his opponents, but it is not his habit to treat people in need in this fashion. This kind of behavior does not fit the image Christians have always had of their Lord and Savior. Not surprisingly, many attempts have been made to soften these strange words of Jesus to the woman. One such attempt that is rather popular today is that Jesus is "testing" the faith of this woman. Conversely, some refuse to rehabilitate Jesus, making him into a racist. The key to this questionable phrase may lie in a *theological* interpretation of the entire story. Let us take the woman's address to Jesus in verse 28 as an example. Whether her address is translated as "a polite sir" (as in the NRSV) or as "a confessional Lord" (the Greek word *kyrie* can render both) will greatly affect the way the entire story is read. If the latter, the story moves from the horizon of the historical Jesus to the time of the early Church, a Church now grappling with the crucial issue of the mission to the Gentiles.

2. *From a miracle story to a theological encounter.* The dialogue between Jesus and the woman (vv. 27–28) transforms this miracle story into a theological encounter between the Risen Lord Jesus and a Gentile woman debating the present access of Gentiles to God's salvation. The use of the bread metaphor not only links the story with the previous chapters but also looks forward to the second feeding story (in the Gentile region of the Decapolis) as well as to the now familiar misunderstanding of the disciples over the loaves (8:17–21). The timeline envisaged by Jesus is not the same timeline envisaged by the woman in this story. While she does not question the priority of Jesus' mission to the children (of Israel), she does state her case that there is bread also for us now! Were there not twelve baskets left, after the five thousand were fed? At stake here is not the future mission to the Gentiles, as Jesus would have it (Let us first . . .), but the woman's conviction that salvation should be made available already now to her people. One can only surmise that—even after the conflicts over the entry of

the Gentiles in the early Church—the community to which Mark is writing needed to be reminded of what Jesus had said and done on this issue. Jesus had not only removed obstacles to the Gentile mission by declaring "all food clean" (7:19), but had also, upon the urging of a Gentile woman, moved resolutely into Gentile territory.

3. *Taking the woman's vision seriously.* In bibles and commentaries, verse 31 is generally seen as introducing Jesus' excursion into Gentile territory where he heals a deaf man (7:32–37) and feeds a crowd of 4000 (8:1–11)—before returning by boat to what appears to be the Jewish side of the lake (8:12). Its connection to the previous story should not, however, be dismissed lightly. Verse 31 not only forms a clear inclusio with verse 24—rounding up the story so to speak—but has Jesus acting immediately upon what he has just learned from the woman ("For saying that . . ."). In a rather surprising move—which scholars generally ascribe to Mark's weak sense of geography of the area—Jesus leaves the region of Tyre by way of Sidon up north, before coming south again towards the east side of the sea of Galilee—always in Gentile territory. This makes little sense geographically, but is quite significant theologically.

Pastoral and homiletical notes

1. *Thematic connection.* Only users of the *Revised Common Lectionary* will read the story of the Syrophoenician woman and that of the deaf mute man as the proposed Gospel reading for this day (Proper 17). While the two stories are different, they can be connected thematically—perhaps using verse 31 as the hinge. Although the *Roman Catholic Lectionary* selection omits the first pericope, preachers would do well to show this same thematic connection between the two stories.

2. *Preaching on the first reading?* The text from Proverbs has little, if anything, to do, thematically or otherwise, with the Gospel story of the Syrophoenician woman. If used as first reading, preachers might have to choose between the two. These words of wisdom are more easily connected to the psalms of the day, 125 or 146.

3. *New ways of being Church!* The move to Gentiles was clearly no easy task for the early communities. Practical difficulties—some of which are reflected in the first part of Mark 7—created a real crisis in the Jesus movement. Paul, in some of his letters (Galatians, Romans, Philippians), and the book of Acts are our primary witnesses to the struggles that faced the Church as it became increasingly challenged (by the Spirit?) to open its doors to the Gentile world. It would appear that things are not so different in our Churches of today. It has always been, and remains, quite a challenge for the Church or Churches to open to new ideas, new visions, new realities, and new ways of being church. Some might be tempted to say that churches should spend more time looking outward than inward, looking out for the other, the world, rather than looking in to our internal problems. Others will retort that our own churches are already filled with "others" that need our immediate attention and acceptance.

25. Twenty-Fourth Sunday in Ordinary Time
Proper 19
Year B

<table>
<tr><td align="center">Roman Catholic L
Isaiah 50:4–9a
Mark 8:27–35</td><td align="center">Revised Common L
Isaiah 50:4–9a
Mark 8:27–38</td></tr>
</table>

The Cost of Following a Suffering Messiah
(Mark 8:27–38)

On Isaiah 50:4–9a

In Isaiah 40—55, a section of Isaiah generally ascribed to the exilic period, an unknown prophet says that God is about to create "new things." God will create an even more extraordinary Exodus, one that will see the return of the people to their homeland. From chapter 49 onwards, the enthusiastic oracles of the first chapters (40—48), give way, however, to a gloomier picture. The initial hope of this great divinely led return from Babylon has proved very different from expectations. This sullen context appears more suitable to at least three of the four so-called Servant songs (42:1–4; 49:1–6; 50:4–9; and 52:13—53:12), in which opposition to, and suffering of, a mysterious "servant" will be instrumental in the liberation of Israel. Today's first reading, the third of these poems, has two different parts. In the first, the servant himself speaks both to his "call" and the opposition and suffering it brings about (vv. 4–6). In the second (vv. 7–9), he expresses his total trust and confidence in God who sustains him in this trial and who will ultimately vindicate his faithful servant.

On Mark 8:27–38
Context

The central section of Mark's Gospel is framed by two healing stories in which Jesus opens the eyes of people who are blind (8:22–26 and

10:45–52). The first of these, a surprisingly "gradual" restoration of a man's sight, creates a bridge between Jesus' activities in Galilee (1:14—8:21) and his journey towards Jerusalem (8:27—10:52). More significantly, it connects the healing and teaching activity of Jesus to the mystery of the cross, soon to be depicted in the second half of Mark's narrative. Set at the very beginning of this crucial section of the Gospel, this healing of a blind person may symbolically point to the disciples' slow process of understanding the mystery of the Christ. As readers will soon discover, Peter, the Twelve, then James and John, will have only a partial vision of the Christ, seeing him at this stage of the narrative more like a "walking tree" (8:24). The section will close with the example of Bartimaeus' total recovery of his sight (understanding) and decision to follow Jesus "on the way" (10:46–52).

Questions

1. Where before in Mark's Gospel did people question the identity of Jesus in this way (8:28) and what did they say about it?
2. Can Peter's confession be separated from Jesus' rebuke of his disciples (vv. 31–33)?
3. Who do you think these "human things" are that Jesus refers to in verse 33?
4. How do you read Jesus' pronouncements in 8:34–35 and are they Good News to you?

⇥ ❦ ❧ ⇤

5. How frequently and where is the title "Christ" used in the Gospel of Mark?
6. Where has Jesus "rebuked" someone or something before in this Gospel? Do you think Jesus is guilty of demonizing Peter and the others in verse 33?
7. What does the change of audience in verse 34 imply about discipleship?
8. Can you think of ways that the words of verses 31 and 34–35 could be used to oppress?

Interpretive points

1. *Partial sight.* Compared to popular opinions concerning Jesus, Peter's answer may be seen as a remarkable confession. This is not, however,

the end of this story. Peter follows his confession with a motion of censure against Jesus' "mission" in Jerusalem, only to be rebuked by Jesus for seeing things the human way. Whatever truth his confession contains, Peter is merely part way there. His understanding is only a partial view of the Messiah Jesus is.

2. *Giving up the power game.* There is an unmistakable change taking place at 8:31. Up to this point, readers may have had the impression that the Jesus of the first half of the Gospel could do anything, even getting the best of his opponents. All this comes to a halt in 8:31, when Jesus, rather unexpectedly, begins to talk about his upcoming journey to Jerusalem and the suffering and death that he will undergo in that city. This new discourse stuns Peter and the other disciples, whose rejection of a suffering Messiah leaves little doubt about the kind of Messiah they wish Jesus to be. This Messiah is no doubt more in line with the powerful Jesus of the first half of Mark's Gospel. The disciples are symbolically blind to the mystery of the cross (8:22–26). With eyes still closed to this mystery, they risk losing themselves in the "power game" caused by their misreading of the "Jesus of power" who has issued loud and clear from Mark 1—8.

3. *Why was Jesus crucified?* Ultimately, Jesus' teaching and actions had political implications. They threatened the system. Things will be no different for his followers. Like Jesus, if they speak and act in the public arena governed by ruthless powers, they too will become a threat to the system. Anyone who is a true follower of the God of Jesus will face costly consequences. To conform and avoid such a cost is a temptation that all followers of Christ will one day or another have to face.

Pastoral and homiletical notes

1. *Like Jesus, like disciples.* The lectionary decision to combine two passages (8:27–34 and 8:34–9:1), which are generally separated in our Bibles, is not without merits. As was claimed earlier in this commentary, Mark's narrative is the story of both Jesus and the disciples. What is said of Jesus will have direct implications for those choosing to "follow after him."

2. *Still much learning to do.* Whatever amount of truth Peter's confession holds, it would be falsifying Mark's Gospel to ignore the subsequent misunderstanding of Peter (and the others). Mark 8:27–33 forms a unit that cannot be separated. Nor, for that matter, should it be isolated from the following instructions on discipleship (8:34—9:1). In that respect, the inclusion of some of these verses in the lectionaries was a wise decision. Preachers cannot miss the connection between the story of Jesus and that of his followers.

3. *Resisting suffering.* Preachers should be conscious of what the words, "You must deny yourself, take up your cross, and follow [Jesus] me," conjure up in the minds of a lot of people today. Jesus did everything to alleviate the suffering of others. His fight against exclusivity, marginality, and abuses brought suffering to his person but he, in no way, endorsed suffering for its own sake. In fact, he spent his life fighting against it.

4. *Who do you say that I am?* This Christological question continues to be asked, studied, and deepened in a variety of contexts and settings. To the Jesus Seminar, recovery of the historical/real Jesus seems more important than what the evangelists have said and made of him. On another front, the universal significance of Christ in God's plan of salvation is raising questions of crucial importance for Churches engaged in dialogue with a world that is becoming increasingly postmodern, pluralistic, and postcolonial. It may be wise to remember that, here in Mark 8, the Christological question (Who do people say that I am?) follows the highly symbolic story of Jesus' progressive healing of the blind person. Full vision is not automatic.

26. Twenty-Fifth Sunday in Ordinary Time
Proper 20
Year B

Roman Catholic L
Wisdom 2:12, 17–20
Mark 9:30–37

Revised Common L
Proverbs 31:10–31
Mark 9:30–37

MORE INSTRUCTIONS ABOUT DISCIPLESHIP
(MARK 9:30–37)

ON WISDOM 2:12, 17–20

As noted earlier, the book of Wisdom begins with exhortations to live righteous lives, which, for the author, is the only road to immortality (1:1–15). These exhortations are followed by what in the end is a sharp denunciation of the "wicked" whose lives lead to death (2:21–24). Before this judgment is issued, however, readers are let into the minds of the wicked, so to speak. They hear of the sad and hopeless state of their lives (2:1–5). This leads them, first, to abandon themselves to lives of pleasure, "because it is our lot" (vv. 6–9) and second, to take pleasure in oppressing the (righteous) poor, the widow, and the weak of society, and third, to make their power the "law of right" (vv. 10–11).

The verses, assigned for today's reading, show the great annoyance of the wicked with "righteous people." They are a threat to their hedonistic ways. What they find particularly "inconvenient" is their judgment, contempt, righteousness, and forbearance. Tormenting and finally getting rid of the "righteous" is a way to test both their fortitude and the God they rely upon! The author's negative judgment (vv. 21–24) concludes his diatribe against the "wicked."

On Mark 9:30–37
Context

The first passion prediction unit (8:31—9:1) was followed by the story of the Transfiguration (9:2–13), the selection for the Second Sunday of Lent, and by the account of the disciples' inability to heal a boy possessed with a mute spirit (vv. 14–29). This last episode forms the immediate context for the second passion prediction unit. This second prediction, as with the first, will be followed by the disciples' inability, perhaps even unwillingness, to grasp Jesus' teaching and further instructions about discipleship (9:35–50).

Questions

1. Does the text provide any reason why Jesus would try at this point to avoid recognition, in Galilee of all places?
2. What do you think makes the disciples fearful of asking Jesus to clarify this second prediction of his passion, death, and resurrection?
3. What theological function does the "house" serve throughout Mark's narrative?

⊷ ❦ ❦ ⊶

4. Why do you think readers are informed twice that the dispute of the disciples over greatness has taken place "on the way" (vv. 33–34)? What greatness are they arguing about?
5. Why do you think Jesus' instructions in verse 35 are addressed specifically to the Twelve?
6. How does Jesus begin to redefine greatness in this passage?

Interpretive points

1. *Instructions for the Twelve.* Contrary to the first passion prediction unit, Jesus' instructions here look more like a collection of disparate sayings, collated to form a so-called mini-catechism on discipleship. One may wonder why this mini-catechism would be addressed specifically to the Twelve, and not again to "the crowd and the disciples" as before in 8:34. One possibility would be that the Twelve stand for the leadership in Mark's community. Jesus' instructions make more sense if

they are addressed to (Christian) leaders. The Twelve were arguing about status, rank, and standing! Jesus reverses this vision of power, turning their thoughts upside down. You want to be first in the community, then you must learn to be "last of all and at the service of all," especially the most vulnerable of society—the children in our midst. To follow Jesus "on the way" is not to think of power, rank, or status. It is to care for society's defenseless legion of "children" as Jesus has done and professes God to do (v. 37).

2. *To be the last of all.* The above interpretation is at variance with the more traditional way of understanding the child as a model or example for Christian discipleship. This may be the meaning of 10:13–16 where disciples are invited to receive or experience the basileia as children. In the context of this passage, Jesus uses the term "child" to teach the disciples of their responsibility to care for the most vulnerable of society. Part of the confusion stemming from this different usage comes from the fact that the Twelve are being called upon to be "last of all." The disciples are disputing among themselves issues of rank, status, and authority. Jesus tries to teach them that authority does not entail rank and status, but rather service. What a paradox! The "child" in this passage cannot model the kind of service Jesus is referring to. To be "last of all" is to be in the service of the "child," those who possess no social status or legal rights, the vulnerable of society. To welcome this "child" is indeed to welcome Jesus and the God he professes.

3. *Called to service.* It is symptomatic of a serious problem for Jesus to call to service the very people who are ticketed for leadership roles by the community. This problem will become even clearer when Jesus instructs the Twelve, following the third and last passion prediction (10:42–45). During this time of chaos and conflict within Mark's community, the leaders themselves now appear confused concerning their role and what that role entails.

Pastoral and homiletical notes

1. *A difficult Messiah to follow.* For a second time, the disciples, here specifically the Twelve, fail to understand, still less accept Jesus' teach-

ing about the cross. Whatever the reason for this second account of their failure, it serves as a warning to readers of the difficulty in understanding and following a suffering Messiah.

2. *The way to life.* Jesus' instructions to the Twelve are reminiscent of instructions from chapter 30 of the book of Deuteronomy. Choose life, not death. Choose the way that leads to life, not the way to death. Yet, for Mark, the way to life leads to death and through death to resurrection and new life. Preachers will recall that for the author of Wisdom, it was righteousness that led to life or immortality (Wis 1:13).

3. *A Christian reading.* The Wisdom text, assigned for this Sunday, may have been chosen to foreshadow or anticipate the sufferings of the innocent Jesus, the Messiah. To avoid any confusion, preachers should ensure that this Christian reading is perceived as but one valid reading of what is essentially a Jewish text.

4. *Ready to serve to the death.* This chapter was written a week or so after John Paul II's last Consistory. In his address, he issued a strong warning to the newly elected cardinals that their mission should be not to pursue careerism but to serve society's most vulnerable, if need be, to the limit of martyrdom. These words of a then dying pope are an excellent commentary on the response of Jesus, on the way to Jerusalem, to the Twelve's dispute about rank, status, and power.

27. Twenty-Sixth Sunday in Ordinary Time
Proper 21
Year B

Roman Catholic L	*Revised Common L*
Numbers 11:25–29	Numbers 11:4–6, 10–16, 24–29
Mark 9:38–43, 45, 47–48	Mark 9:38–50

Still More Instructions "on the Way"
(Mark 9:38–50)

On Numbers 11:25–29

The books of Exodus and Numbers recount that Israel's odyssey in the desert was marked by a lot of murmuring against the Lord, their liberator, and Moses, their leader. Numbers 11 provides a good example. It begins with the people complaining about their misfortunes, quickly discarded and punished harshly by the Lord (11:1–3). More protest from the people, this time about their daily diet (vv. 4–9), again stirs up the Lord's anger. This anger annoys Moses who issues his own grievance to the Lord's about the heavy burden of having to lead alone "all this people" (vv. 10–15). In response, the Lord instructs Moses to co-opt the help of seventy acknowledged elders, who will be given their share of Moses' spirit (vv. 16–23).

Today's selection reports how these instructions to Moses were carried out. As promised (v. 17), the Lord takes some of the spirit that is on Moses and puts it on the seventy elders, empowering them to prophesy, but only for this one occasion (v. 25). Two elders, who have remained in the camp, also receive their share of the spirit given to Moses, and are reported to prophesy. Joshua, seemingly overprotecting of his leader (v. 29), disapproves. Moses, on the contrary, wishes that all the Lord's people were prophets! Is the purpose of this episode simply to hail the prophetic charisma or to claim its independence from any earthly institutional controls?

On Mark 9:38–50
Context

Today's selection concludes one of the longest teaching sections of the Gospel of Mark. It began with the second passion prediction (9:30), was followed by the dispute of the Twelve over who was greatest, and continued with Jesus' corrective instructions to the Twelve about authority as service to the vulnerable. The second half of this teaching segment again starts with the Twelve's difficulty to understand the actions of the "strange exorcist" (vv. 38–41) and, as before, is followed by more teaching about discipleship (vv. 42–50). Although this conversation takes place in a house in Capernaum (v. 33), readers will remember that it is also happening "on the way" to Jerusalem (9:33–34).

Questions

1. Why do you think John and the other disciples are so annoyed that an outsider is casting out demons in Jesus' name?
2. To whom are the instructions found in verses 41–42 and 43–50 addressed?
3. Is there a difference between the warning Jesus gives in verse 42 and those found in verses 43–48?

⊱ ❦ ❦ ⊰

4. Who are the "little ones who believe in me" in verse 42? Do you think that they could be related to the "children" of verse 37?
5. How should the warnings of verses 43–48 be understood in our Churches of today?
6. How do you understand Jesus' statement in verse 49 in terms of purification or some kind of punishment?

Interpretive points

1. *Astounding deafness.* In 9:33–34, the Twelve were arguing among themselves about rank and status. Here, in 9:38, John and his companions (see the thrice-repeated use of "we" and "us" in this verse) are angry at the intrusion of an outsider into their group (he was not following us). To have an outsider casting out demons "in Jesus' name" is to en-

croach on their rights and privileges as disciples. Jesus again admonishes them for their attitude and states that "Whoever is not against us is for us." Somewhat ironically, the episode harks back to the disciples' own failure to cast out a demon in 9:14–29. Acting in Jesus' name is not exclusive to any one community or leader. Inclusiveness, not exclusiveness, should be the mark of followers of Jesus. It may be added that such frequent references to the Twelve's astounding deafness has the rhetorical effect of better informing readers of who Jesus really is and what it means to be his followers. To paraphrase a scholar, every time the disciples need a little more instruction, readers get some too (Struthers Malbon, *Hearing Mark*, 65).

2. *Who are the addressees?* Mark 9:42–48 (even 49–50) contains various sayings, generally believed to have circulated in the early Church, perhaps independently and without their present narrative context. Here, they are linked by the catchword "stumbling block" and its composites. Once imported in the framework of Mark's story, this collection of sayings serves the context in which they are now located. The audience has not changed. Jesus still addresses the Twelve, the very ones called to a leadership of service. Few commentators deal squarely with the question of audience, speaking simply of discipleship. As in 9:35–37, in this new context, the words of Jesus are addressed not to disciples in general, but more specifically to the Twelve.

3. *Two very different warnings.* The use of the verb "stumble" or "be an obstacle to" (*skandalizein*) links the warnings Jesus makes in verse 42 and in verses 43–48. The warnings themselves, however, have little to do with one another. In verse 42, the warning to the Twelve is against becoming obstacles to the little ones "who believe in Jesus." The Twelve must be careful not to abuse their authority and lead "weaker" members of their community astray. Whatever "scandal" this may cause, its punishment leaves no doubt about its gravity. Conversely, in verses 43–48, Jesus moves into a new direction, inviting the same Twelve to look within and rid themselves of anything that might hamper their leadership. In the present narrative context, the "temptations" that may cause the Twelve to stumble would appear to concern their interest in status and their exclusiveness. The seriousness

of this matter for Jesus is conveyed by his use of hyperboles, cutting off one's hand or foot, and tearing one's eyes out, and his reference to the unquenchable fire of hell awaiting whoever fails to remove obstacles that might cause them to abuse their authority.

Pastoral and homiletical notes

1. *Remember the Twelve?* If our suggestion that the Twelve, and what they stand for, are the primary recipients of these instructions of Jesus is correct, preachers will do well to acknowledge this reality before applying them to all disciples.

2. *No exclusivism.* The episode of the excluded exorcist (vv. 38–41) might be a good starting point for a reflection or sermon on the ever-present temptation to exclude the "other" from our faith communities.

3. *Avoiding the temptation of moralizing.* Preachers should not minimize the traumatic impact of this reading, verses 42–48 in particular, on many of our Christians. The prospect of everlasting punishment will evoke times past when similar words or images may have been used to manipulate and control. What is more urgently needed is a more open theological approach to the God Jesus presents us with in our reading today.

4. *Trusting God's spirit.* The account of Numbers 11 and the story of the "strange exorcist" (Mark 9:38–40) illustrate the same thematic theme. In both cases, Moses and Jesus trust the work of the "spirit" and encourage their followers to do the same.

28. TWENTY-SEVENTH SUNDAY IN ORDINARY TIME
PROPER 22
Year B

Roman Catholic L	***Revised Common L***
Genesis 2:18–24	Genesis 2:18–24
Mark 10:2–16	Mark 10:2–16

TEACHING ABOUT DIVORCE AND REMARRIAGE
(MARK 10:2–16)

ON GENESIS 2:18–24

The purpose of this etiological story is to account for human existence—woman and man—as intended by God. The earth creature (Heb *ha'adam*) is put to sleep by God. On waking up after surgery, the creature discovers that he is a man (Heb *ish*) in the presence of a woman (Heb *issha*). So attractive is this woman that a man will leave the home of his father and mother to cling to her as his wife. Verse 25—which is not included in today's selection—speaks to the perfect harmony between woman and man. With this harmony broken in Genesis 3, they will feel the need to put "cloths" on, no longer completely at ease with each other (3:7).

ON MARK 10:2–16
Context

Jesus is on the move again and his direction is south-southwest, decidedly on his way to Jerusalem. To reach that city from Galilee, Jesus and the disciples, like most Jews of the time, take a longer route through the Jordan valley in order to avoid the territory of the Samaritans. Large crowds soon flock around Jesus and, as always, he teaches them. Some Pharisees arrive on the scene and present a challenge to Jesus. The disciples are not far away and observe the interaction.

Questions

1. To whom do you think are these words of Jesus directed, oppressors or victims of oppression?
2. How do you interpret Jesus' answer in verses 6–9? Is he forbidding divorce and remarriage under any circumstances?
3. Do you think Jesus is abrogating part of the Torah (Deut 24:1–4) with his stand on divorce?

⊷ ❦ ❧ ⊶

4. Compare Mark 10:1–12 with its parallel in Matthew 19:3–9 and identify the main difference with regard to the prohibition. In your view, do Genesis 1:27 and 2:24 address the divisive issues that arise in human relationships after the fall has occurred?
5. Is Jesus in 10:11–12 making of divorce and remarriage a "violation of the Decalogue prohibition of adultery"? If so, on what basis is this sin still deemed unforgivable in some Churches?
6. What do you think might have prompted such an account in the context of Mark's community: a dangerous situation that called for "legislation" or a pastoral problem that needed attention?

Interpretive points

1. *Does Jesus forbid divorce and remarriage?* Is it lawful for a man to divorce his wife? The question is puzzling on the lips of these Pharisees. To our best knowledge, divorce was accepted as a reality in first-century Judaism. There was a big debate, however, concerning the grounds for divorce—illustrated by the Pharisees' different question in Matthew's parallel account: "Is it lawful for a man to divorce his wife *for any cause?*" (19:3)

   Contrary to Matthew, the controversy in Mark is not over the grounds for divorce, but over the very issue of divorce. The "test" to which Jesus is subjected is not about which side of the current debate he is on, but about whether divorce is permitted at all in the Torah ("Is it lawful for a man . . . ?"). Taking their clue from Jesus' reference to the Torah, these Pharisees reply, rightly so, that Moses "allowed" a man to legally divorce his wife by providing her with a letter of dismissal. In his reply, Jesus attributes this "commandment" permitting divorce to the sclerosis of their heart. But in God's original design, things were not so.

What is remarkable about Jesus' answer is not his reference to creation, to how things were in the beginning (Gen 1:27 and 2:24), but his inference from God's original design on woman and man: "Therefore what God has joined together, let no one separate" (10:9). Scholars generally agree that with this phrase—which is not part of Genesis 2:24—Jesus is actually prohibiting divorce in Mark and, if his further explanations to the disciples "in the house" are taken into view (vv. 11–12), also remarriage. Most interpreters, at this point, appear quite satisfied with what they describe as the Markan Jesus' absolute prohibition of divorce. Most, however, are also quick to bring into view the two notable exceptions from Paul (1 Cor 7:10–16) and Matthew (5:32 and 19:9) which seem to allow for a more caring and "gracious" pastoral practice.

2. *Ideal world vs. real world.* How should Jesus' absolute prohibition of divorce be understood today: as an ideal or as a law or prescription? If viewed as a law, what then about the real world? If Jesus' vision and sanction of God's original design on woman and man is prescriptive, a law to be observed with sanctions, where does that leave Christian women and men whose marriages are, for whatever reasons, broken, dead, and no longer viable?

The first two chapters of the book of Genesis, which provides the first reading for this Sunday (Gen 2:18–24), depict an "ideal world" where everything is good and harmonious. The real world, full of disharmony and violence, begins with Genesis 3 and its description of the "fall." It is with this real world—our world—that God has struck a covenant: first with Noah and his family (Gen 9), then with the family of Abraham and Sarah (Gen 12), and finally with a stiff-necked Israel (Exod 34, not Exod 19—24). For Christians, who are the beneficiaries of God's new covenant in Christ?

By harking back to God's original design of woman and man, Jesus returns to the *ideal* world of Genesis 1—2. For what purpose, one may ask? By inferring that such a design includes the prohibition of divorce ("therefore let no one separate what God has joined together"), Jesus appears to be moving beyond the text of Genesis. Furthermore, his conclusion does not take into account the *real world*, the world after Genesis 3—full of disharmony and violence. Could it be the purpose of Jesus' private instruction to his disciples to clarify this very point? According to Jesus (vv. 11–21), whoever divorces and marries another person commits adultery towards the first spouse. Adultery is included among the evil intentions that come from the human heart in 7:22. It shares the field with "fornication, theft, murder, avarice, wickedness, deceit, licentiousness, envy, slander, pride and folly." Are any of these "evil intentions" deemed unforgivable? Let us recall once more the example of the disciples in Mark. In spite of their hardness of heart (6:52 and 8:18), Jesus continues to call them into a deeper understanding of the *basileia*. Even after their betrayal, he follows on his promise to look after them (14:28 and 16:7). Failures, compassion, forgiveness, and grace are part and parcel of the *basileia* that Jesus calls his disciples into. Just as they continue to live in the "already-but-not-yet-present" *basileia*, so do Christian communities today. We can, and unfortunately do at times, harden our hearts and act as if we are already living in the ideal world of the *basileia*, in a world where there is only peace and harmony. We know that this is not our world. In this world where discord and disharmony in relationships often occur, what are we to understand from these words of Jesus? Are they calling us, as Christian communities, to judge or exclude people because of divorce?

Pastoral and homiletical notes

1. *Churches' discipline.* Where does your Church or denomination stand on the question of divorce and remarriage? Can you reconcile the above text (and its interpretation) with such a policy? Support it with Church statements or guidelines.

2. *Contextualized reading.* Because of today's greater sensitivity to the pastoral situation of divorced and remarried people, it is urgent to seek ways to read this and other texts in dialogue with and through the lens of our contemporary situations. Was the above interpretation of this passage helpful to address this sensitive pastoral issue?

3. *Apostolic interpretations?* Is it possible to preach on this text without keeping before our eyes and our congregations the "interpretations" of Matthew and Paul?

4. *Unforgivable sin?* Someone whose husband had just left her for another woman was reported as saying: "In the Catholic Church, you can kill someone, go to confession, and again be able to receive communion. But for people who are divorced and have remarried, this is not possible." How is one to respond to that?

29. Twenty-Eighth Sunday in Ordinary Time
Proper 23
Year B

<table>
<tr><td align="center">Roman Catholic L
Wisdom 7:7–11
Mark 10:17–30</td><td align="center">Revised Common L
Job 23:1–9, 16–17
Mark 10:17–31</td></tr>
</table>

Teaching about Wealth and Possessions
(Mark 10:17–30)

On Wisdom 7:7–11

The author of the book of Wisdom writes to a Jewish community under attack by the alienating culture of the Empire. He follows his demonstration of the superiority of a life of righteousness over the life of pleasure, power, and injustice promoted by the "wicked" (1–6:21), with a long persuasive argument for the pursuit of Wisdom that comes from God (6:22—11:1). Harking back to a tradition well known to his readers, the author uses the first person, a Solomon revived (1 Kgs 3—4), to praise, pray and search for true Wisdom. He appears to be using Solomon's life, guided by God's wisdom, as a deliberate contrast to the philosophy of life of the "wicked" (chapter 2).

Today's reading follows a brief reflection on the mortal condition shared by all humans, even kings like Solomon (7:1–6). Yet, contrary to the self-indulged way of life chosen by the wicked, the king prays for, and is given, the Wisdom of God to guide his whole life (v. 7). He prefers "her" to everything else, all the goods most cherished by humans: power and wealth (v. 8), riches (v. 9), health, beauty, and light (v. 10). Ironically, all these goods will come to him through Wisdom—the mother of them all (vv. 11–12).

ON MARK 10:17–30
Context

Jesus and his disciples, continuing their journey toward Jerusalem (v. 17), are still presumably in the region of Judea, near or beyond the Jordan (10:1). Jesus' encounter with the man of "many possessions" and the teaching that follows conclude a set of instructions begun in 10:1. This episode, like the previous two on divorce (vv. 2–12) and the children (vv. 13–16), begins with an issue formulated in narrative form (vv. 17–22)—what is needed to have eternal life. It ends with significant words from Jesus about wealth, possessions (vv. 23–27), and family (vv. 28–31).

Questions

1. What has the text to say about the man's search and why do you think he is coming to Jesus?
2. Do you think that Jesus' request of the rich man to sell what he owns and give the money to the poor is part of what is necessary for all to inherit eternal life or is the mark of a special calling to walk with him?
3. In what way do the last verses (28–31) contribute to resolving the initial question of the rich man?

$\longmapsto$ ❦ ❦ $\longmapsto$

4. Do you notice anything peculiar in the list of commandments recited by Jesus that might point to the systemic evil of wealth?
5. What do you make of Jesus' "social analysis" of wealth and of his solution (vv. 17–22)?
6. What do you think of the reactions of the disciples to Jesus' comments on the difficulty for rich people to experience the *basileia* (vv. 24 and 26)?
7. What do you think the narrative and rhetorical function of verses 23–27 is, especially of verse 27?

Interpretive points

1. *Honoring the man's faithful obedience to God.* The reason for including the stipulation "You shall not defraud" among the Ten Commandments is not obvious. Whatever the reason may be, the man who has

"kept all these commandments since his youth" (v. 20) cannot be accused of misguiding practices in accumulating his wealth (see 11:40–41). To contrast or even oppose the terms of Jesus' invitation with what was required from any observant Jew would, therefore, be tantamount to dishonoring the man's faithful relationship to God—something that Jesus appears not ready to do.

2. *What kind of story is that?* One of the most disputed issues concerning this narrative touches on its genre. Are we in touch with a general teaching or rule of Jesus about discipleship, or rather in the presence of a specific call—like those of the first four disciples and of Levi—to leave everything and follow Jesus? The following dialogue of Jesus with his disciples, especially his response to Peter (vv. 28–31), makes it difficult to understand this story as a general teaching about discipleship.

3. *Nothing is impossible to God!* Jesus' pronouncement should be taken seriously that wealth, or rather an exaggerated attachment to wealth, possessions, and money, may often prove an obstacle to experiencing the *basileia.* These are hard words, but they are not the last words of Jesus on this subject. Wealth may prove to be an obstacle to experiencing the *basileia,* but may not necessarily be insurmountable. "For mortals it is impossible, but not for God; for God all things are possible."

4. *Who then can be saved?* This objection from the disciples harks back to and reflects the positive value attached to wealth and possessions in the Jewish tradition (Sir 11:21–22). Although such a view had been challenged in Job, Qohelet, and elsewhere, it is not clear from the text where Jesus stands on this matter. He seems more interested in warning his disciples of the danger wealth may constitute in one's pursuit or experience of the *basileia.* Mark, unlike Luke, gives no specifics as to how this may or may not happen.

Pastoral and homiletical notes

1. *Experiencing the* basileia *today.* Viewing Mark 10:17–31 as a unit will help preachers focus not only on wealth, but also on what Christian

discipleship might call for in relation to the issue of wealth. Although Jesus' saying to his disciples on the difficulty for those who have wealth to enter the *basileia* points to the end time, preachers will remember that God's *basileia* is already present, though not yet fully, in our midst. In this regard, to speak of experiencing, rather than entering, the *basileia* makes more sense of what one is called to be and to do. Indeed, one can think of various obstacles, not only wealth and possessions, to the way one might experience God's *basileia*.

2. *Respecting Judaism.* With this Gospel passage, preachers have another opportunity to challenge perceptions that, unfortunately, continue to plague Christian consciousness. More specifically, they are encouraged to gradually dispel the supersessionist belief that reduces Judaism to a mere "legalistic religion" in contrast with a more grace-oriented Christianity. It may be healthy to remind us Christians that our own religion, any religion, faces a similar danger. This lamentable "legalistic approach" to religion was most resolutely denounced by Israel's prophets, as epitomized in Hosea 6:6: "For I desire steadfast love and not sacrifice, the knowledge of God rather than burnt offerings."

3. *An inspiring story.* Over the centuries, many people have drawn great inspiration from stories such as the Call of the Rich Man, and accepted to sell everything they had to follow the more radical lifestyle of Jesus.

4. *Pursuing the wisdom of the* basileia. Solomon's pursuit of Wisdom over everything else is echoed in the story of the Rich Man, invited to sell the many possessions he owned and follow Jesus. The reward "in this age" that Jesus promises to those who have left everything to follow him (Mark 10:30) appears to include many of the earthly goods that Solomon is granted through the gift of Wisdom. Yet, this Gospel text, itself, presents wealth and possessions as major obstacles to one's experience of the *basileia*. There appears to be more to the *basileia* than the text, at first glance, implies.

30. Twenty-Ninth Sunday in Ordinary Time
Proper 24
Year B

<table>
<tr><td>Roman Catholic L</td><td>Revised Common L</td></tr>
<tr><td>Isaiah 53:10–11</td><td>Isaiah 53:4–12</td></tr>
<tr><td>Mark 10:35–45</td><td>Mark 10:35–45</td></tr>
</table>

Leadership as Service
(Mark 10:35–45)

On Isaiah 53:4–12

All four "Servant songs" in the second half of the book of Isaiah sketch the figure of a servant and describe his mission and achievements. Building up on the third song, the fourth poem (Is 52:12—53:12), of which today's selection is a part, describes the vicarious suffering and death of this mysterious "servant" and his final vindication and exaltation by God. More than the other three, this fourth song will be familiar to Christians because of the way Jesus has been identified with this "suffering servant" in the Christian tradition. Contrary to the *Revised Common Lectionary*, which includes the greater portion of this fourth Servant song, the Roman Catholic selection has retained only the second and third last verses. Both verses revisit the servant's vicarious mission and his victory, but it is verse 10 that make the important claim that his suffering was willed by the Lord.

On Mark 10:35–45
Context

With today's selection, we reach the third and final major segment of what we earlier have identified as the central section of Mark's Gospel (8:22—10:52). This section, like the first two, centers on Jesus' third passion prediction (10:32–34), followed by the disciples' misunderstanding (10:35–40/41) and then by some remedial teaching by Jesus about discipleship (10:42–45).

Questions

1. How would you characterize the request of James and John and why do you think the Ten are angry with them?
2. In order to understand the thrust of Jesus' instructions in verses 43–45, how significant is it to identify the audience to which he speaks?
3. In light of the original meaning of the Greek verb "to serve at table" (*diakonein*), what revolutionary understanding of service is here proposed by Jesus?

✻ ❦ ✻

4. What is the function, both narrative and rhetorical, of verse 45 and what does it add to Jesus' previous instructions in 9:35–36?
5. What historical situation or issue in Mark's community do you think these words of Jesus are addressing?
6. Do you think Jesus' understanding of the term "service" has any bearing on how the same term is used of women in 1:31 and 15:41?

Interpretive points

1. *Instruction for leaders.* Surprisingly, most commentators fail to raise the question of audience at this point, apparently content to interpret this episode as one more example of some global discipleship instructions by Jesus. Yet, there are several indications that this exhortation to act as "servants" is not likely addressed to those whose expected social role is already to "serve," like slaves and women, but more specifically to those who, like the Twelve, are or will be in position of power or authority. First, the Twelve are singled out in verse 32 and, once more (see 9:32–34), made privy to the third and final prediction of the passion, death, and resurrection of Jesus. Second, here, their expected behavior is contrasted with the way Gentiles exercise power and authority over their subjects. Third, Jesus' teaching is addressed to those "among you" who wish "to become great" or "to be first." Last, Jesus offers his own example of "service" and "giving his own life" as a model to be fol-

lowed. To read these words of Jesus in terms of equality among members of the community rather than specific teaching to the Twelve concerning leadership, may be letting a "leadership" off the hook that, up to now, has all too often been thinking status, prestige, and power.

2. *Leadership of service.* The final section of the passage (10:41–45) contrasts two visions of power, two perceptions or understandings of the way power and authority are to be exercised. Over and against the way Gentile rulers "lord" over and tyrannize their people, Jesus warns his chosen Twelve that to achieve greatness and precedence, presumably in the *basileia*, they must follow his example. They must become slaves and servants to their fellow believers. This revolutionary prescription for future leaders leads one to suspect that the Twelve, also perhaps the leadership of the community, have yet to grasp the meaning of Jesus' life and death. They still think prestige, power, and glory, rather than service and humility.

3. *Not to be served but to serve!* Mark's narrative never portrays Jesus "serving at table," the primary meaning of the Greek term *diakonein*. Mark does present him, no less than three times, as the recipient of the "service" of angels (1:13), of some women disciples from Galilee (15:41), and of Peter's mother-in-law (1:31). Mark 10:45a is the sole instance of the category "service" being used to define or explain Jesus' mission. Therefore, in order to understand what "service" means in the context of this story, we must look back at how Jesus defines "service" in his life and ministry in the first half of the Gospel, a ministry that the Twelve themselves were commissioned to embrace (6:7–13). In light of their performance in Mark, it would appear that women such as the hemorrhaging woman, the woman from Syrophoenicia, and the anointing woman may be the very ones embodying "service" as it is defined by Jesus. They all, in their own way, understand the true nature of the mission of Jesus. Despite the dangers entailed, they all reach out to Jesus and express their belief and faith in that mission. Interestingly, their true discipleship may also explain their curious absence in this central section of Mark's narrative (8:27—10:52) perhaps, because whenever they appear they embody what apparently is so lacking in the Twelve.

4. *Give his life a ransom for many.* Dark images of a required sacrifice, a price to be paid, sins to be atoned for, and a "sadistic" God bidding the death of his own son have filled the minds of Christians for centuries and make more than a few of us uncomfortable today. Is it possible to understand the death of Jesus as Mark does, without yielding to the image or vision of a sadistic God demanding to be appeased or placated? The first explanation that this Gospel provides of the significance of the death of Jesus (for the second, see 14:24) cannot be separated from Jesus' statement about his mission. Jesus' death was the outcome of his life, of his faithfulness to his vision of God's *basileia.* A Jesus, unwilling to bear the consequences of his beliefs to the end, would make little sense. In this respect, it makes sense to speak of Jesus sacrificing himself or his life, of paying a price not to God, but to proclaim God's justice and love in the world. Like Jesus, and also John the Baptist (10:38), the Twelve must be willing and ready, as "servants" and "slaves" to all, to endure suffering and even death.

    To many critics, the above reading does not do full justice to Mark's claim that Jesus came "to give his life [as] a ransom for many," because it fails to take into account what they see as a universal and unique dimension to Jesus' death, reaching far beyond the death of any martyrs for a cause, ancient and contemporary. Interestingly, two very different Scripture models will ground these two very different interpretations. The model I propose is grounded in the martyrdom of the seven brothers in the first and fourth books of Maccabees (1 Mac 2:50 and 6:44 and 4 Mac 17:20–22). The model of the universal and unique Jesus is grounded in the story of the Suffering Servant of Isaiah 53. Restriction of space prevents us from giving any further attention to this fascinating discussion. However, it is important to note that more than one interpretation of the death of Jesus exists and is rooted in our Scriptural texts.

Pastoral and homiletical notes

1. *Importance of context.* Since today's lectionary selection omits the narrative setting of this Gospel reading, preachers will do well to ensure that congregations hear the narrative context. Since Jesus' life and death lie at the very foundation of his teaching on service and the

gift of one's life, congregations need to hear Jesus' third and final prediction of his passion as well as the strange reactions of his followers to it (vv. 32–34). In order to understand how difficult the life of "service" that all disciples are called to, we need to understand clearly that the life and death of Jesus exemplify this service. The "strange reactions" experienced by the Twelve are not so different from the strange reactions many of us experience today.

2. *Authority as service!* It should not be lost that Jesus' instruction on "service" seems to be addressed primarily to the future leaders of the Church. This passage may be a welcome opportunity to reflect out loud, or discuss, with the congregation the way authority or leadership is being exercised in the community and in the Church at large.

3. *The Suffering Servant and the Twelve.* The "hermeneutical" combination of sections of Isaiah 53 and Mark 10:35–45 will influence the interpretation of the death of Jesus in terms of the Suffering Servant. It will also influence the future activity of the Twelve and their representatives who will now be called to be "servants" even unto the death.

31. Thirtieth Sunday in Ordinary Time
Proper 25
Year B

Roman Catholic L	*Revised Common L*
Jeremiah 31:7–9	Jeremiah 31:7–9
Mark 10:46–52	Mark 10:46–52

Following Jesus on the Way
(Mark 10:46–52)

On Jeremiah 31:7–9

Jeremiah 31:7–9 is part of the Book of Consolation (30—33), so called because it contains a collection of oracles of salvation on the restoration of Israel (30—31) and Judah (32—33). These oracles are developed around the prophet's strange purchase of a field in the midst of the Jerusalem siege (32:1–15). They are placed at the center of the book and designed to offer hope to a people in exile.

The short unit of Jeremiah 31:7–9 follows the majestic good news of the Lord's love for, and faithfulness towards, "all the families of Israel" from their first exodus and desert experience to a new exodus about to take place (31:1–6). People are invited to rejoice over the Lord's plan to bring back a remnant from exile (v. 7). This remnant or "great company" will include "the blind and the lame, those with child and those in labor" (v. 8) and, this time says the Lord, the desert will be more hospitable to them (v. 9a). As the prophets interpreted the exile as the act of the Lord, so does Jeremiah interpret their deliverance. God's love for, and faithfulness towards, Israel have not failed (v. 9b).

On Mark 10:46–52
Context

The story of the healing of "blind Bartimaeus" of Jericho brings to a close a journey narrative of Mark that has taken Jesus and the disciples all the way from the northern region of Caesarea Philippi (8:27–30) to the city of Jerusalem. Coming from Galilee (presumably) through the Jordan valley, Jesus and the disciples now enter Jericho, the last town one enters before the difficult climb towards Jerusalem, about 25 kilometers away and some 1000 meters above the valley floor. It is here at Jericho that Jesus and his disciples are soon to be joined by Bartimaeus.

Questions

1. Compare how Bartimaeus is described both at the beginning of the story and, then, at the end.
2. How would you describe this story, a call narrative or a paradigm for following Jesus "on the way"?
3. Do you see any symbolic value in Bartimaeus' action of "throwing off his garment" on his way to Jesus?

4. What do you think the expression "Son of David" means? Has Mark done anything to prepare readers up to this point for this "faith confession" in Jesus?
5. Taking into consideration the entire central section of Mark's narrative, what do you think Bartimaeus is really asking from Jesus? Do you think that the "blindness" of Bartimaeus is in any way related to James and John in 10:36?
6. Do you think this story is about physical healing, spiritual healing, or both?

Interpretive points

1. *Becoming a true disciple.* Hailed as a hermeneutical key to the Gospel of Mark, the healing of blind Bartimaeus owes its popularity to its narrative and theological function in the structure of the Gospel. Read in conjunction with the first healing of a blind person in 8:22–26, Mark helps the reader to focus on spiritual sight and understanding. These two stories of eye opening frame what is viewed as the most important section of the whole Gospel (8:27—10:45). Peter, despite his confession in 8:27 as well as the other disciples do not yet see nor understand what is happening and what being a "follower"

of Jesus really entails. They are like the first blind person whose eyes are being progressively opened (8:22–26). They don't yet see clearly, perhaps because, unlike Bartimaeus, they don't desire to see. Theirs, at this point in the narrative, is only a partial understanding. In contrast to the sons of Zebedee who ask for power and status (10:35–37), the blind Bartimaeus simply wants to see. With his sight immediately and fully restored, he is now the one who sees and understands what "discipleship" entails and still chooses to follow Jesus "on the way."

2. *An ambiguous title?* Bartimaeus' double identification of Jesus as "Son of David" has drawn much attention from scholars, but the discussion has focused almost entirely on historical issues (Was Jesus ever called "Son of David" or why did Jesus not reject the title or check its use as he has done with the Twelve in 8:30?). Of more interest to our analysis is whether this title has any significance in this story. Bartimaeus' double cry constitutes the first instance of the use of this title in Mark's narrative. The evangelist will refer twice more to David in the next two chapters: in the so-called triumphal entry of Jesus into Jerusalem (11:10) and in Jesus' question concerning the usefulness of calling the Messiah "Son of David" (12:35). In both cases there are good reasons to suspect, that for Mark, the messianic or nationalistic overtones attached to this title does not appropriately apply to Jesus. While it does not automatically follow that Bartimaeus' use of this title includes this nationalistic view, one simply cannot dismiss it at this point in the narrative. His restored sight may foreshadow a fuller understanding of both Jesus' mission and the cost of discipleship, but it is not the end of the story. In narrative terms, the full understanding of Jesus will be displayed only at the foot of the cross, with Jesus already dead. For attentive readers (see Mark 1:1), "Son of God," not "Son of David," will then be the title applied to Jesus.

Pastoral and homiletical notes

1. *Physical or spiritual healing?* Focusing solely, or primarily, on the physical healing of Bartimaeus to the detriment of the restoration of his spiritual sight and understanding will disconnect the story from its

narrative context. Preachers may want to again read our earlier comments on miracle stories as parabolic.

2. *Mind the context.* It is well known that lectionary selections are often given, and proclaimed, without their narrative and theological context. This context may not be as urgently required in some cases as it is in others. This is not the case with the story of blind Bartimaeus. As noted above, together with the healing of Bethsaida (8:22–26), this story frames the central section of Mark. Without an explicit reference to its crucial context, preachers will be hard pressed to unveil the symbolic meaning intended by Mark.

3. *A fitting story.* The story of the healing of Bartimaeus and his decision to follow Jesus on the way to Jerusalem is not only a fitting conclusion to the central section of Mark's narrative but also constitutes a suitable conclusion to that section of the lectionary. More, I believe, than any other sections of Mark, Jesus' vital instructions on discipleship, leadership, service, and suffering found in this section, have made it into the lectionary—a direct confirmation of their importance in the eyes of Churches. These instructions are challenging and will be a test for anyone who chooses to commit their lives to the *basileia*. Facing this challenge, many of us may find ourselves as the disciples, narratively portrayed in Mark as slow like the blind man from Bethsaida, unable to see or to grasp Jesus' message. Conversely, as the story of Bartimaeus shows us, for anyone who demands to see, Jesus stands always ready and willing to restore their sight.

4. *One reading of many.* By combining Jesus' healing of blind Bartimaeus with the oracle of Jeremiah 31, the lectionary fosters a Christian reading of a First Testament text. As noted above, Jeremiah 31 is about God's decision to bring back a remnant from exile, a remnant that would include the blind, the lame, and the weak. Preachers choosing to use this hermeneutical frame should remember that a Christian reading is but only one reading among many, and should, therefore, avoid promoting a supersessionist presentation of this Christian message.

32. Thirty-First Sunday in Ordinary Time
Proper 26
Year B

Roman Catholic L
Deuteronomy 6:2–6
Mark 12:28–34

Revised Common L
Deuteronomy 6:1–9
Mark 12:28–34

"You Are Not Far from the Kingdom of God"
(Mark 12:28–34)

On Deuteronomy 6:2–6

The farewell discourse or final words of Moses is a literary fiction, which makes up most of the book of Deuteronomy. It is addressed to a people about to enter the Promised Land (see 6:1). These words, historically, are, in fact, spoken to a people already living in the land. Their purpose is to help these people live among the people of the land of Canaan, without giving way to their "abhorrent practices" (18:9–14).

Today's reading is divided into two distinct parts. The first is a general exhortation to the people by Moses to hear and observe divinely ordained "statutes and ordinances" that will guarantee their prosperity in the land (vv. 1–3). The second distinct part is what is known as the *Shema Israel*, the creed of Judaism to this very day (vv. 4–9). As a restatement, in positive terms, of the first commandment of the Decalogue (5:7; Exod 20:3), this *Shema* (Hebrew for "hear" or "listen") articulates Israel's unique relationship to their God. They must love the Lord their God with all their being (vv. 4–5), internalize the divine words (v. 6), teach them to their children (v. 7), and ritualize them bodily, socially, and within their homes (vv. 8–9).

ON MARK 12:28–34
Context

Today's Gospel selection, Jesus' friendly encounter with one of the scribes, falls in the midst of a series of controversies (11:27—12:37) involving Jesus and what has been called a wide coalition of the most influential people in Jerusalem. These controversies follow on the heels of two dramatic actions by Jesus: the Triumphal Approach to Jerusalem (11:1–11), studied earlier, and the Cleansing of the Temple (11:15–19).

It is this last action of Jesus that appears to cause the coalition of "the chief priests, the scribes, and the elders" to challenge his authority (11:27–33). Following the Parable of the Wicked Tenants (12:1–11), which would have led to his arrest if not for fear of the crowds (v. 12), other members of this united front engage Jesus in controversy. A group of Pharisees and Herodians challenge him over the tribute to Caesar (12:13–17) and some Sadducees, who do not believe in the resurrection of the body, test him on this very question (vv. 18–27). Following our Gospel reading of today, the encounter between Jesus and a rather exceptional scribe, the controversy will continue. Jesus will critique the way scribes read their own Scriptures on the origin of the Messiah (12:35–38), their status-seeking attitude, and oppression of widows (vv. 38–40). These confrontations, with different segments of the Jewish leadership, take place in the Temple area (12:1, 31, 38).

Questions

1. To which passages from the Torah does Jesus appeal to his answer to the scribe's question (vv. 29–31)?
2. How important is what the scribe adds in his response to Jesus?
3. According to the text, what is preventing this scribe from experiencing the *basileia* of God?

⊢— ❦ ❦ —⊣

4. What would you say distinguishes this scribe from the understanding of scribes given up to this point in Mark's narrative?
5. To which prophetic criticism of "worship" does the scribe refer to and what are the implications of such criticism in the immediate context of Mark 11—12?

6. Do you think that the scribe's understanding of neighbor has any-
    thing to do with his understanding of God?

Interpretive points

1. *Avoid stereotyping.* Mark's overwhelmingly hostile stereotyping of the
    scribes contrasts with his unique presentation of this one exceptional
    scribe (he has not come, like in Matthew, to *test* Jesus!). Interpretations
    of the Gospels often present the scribes as a uniform body standing
    always over and against Jesus. This story shatters this typecasting and
    presents us with a more realistic representation of the diversity to be
    found amidst the scribes.

2. *Co-opting the scribe.* The scribe, in response to Jesus, stresses the univer-
    sality of God, "God is one, and besides him there is no other," and the
    superiority of love of God and neighbor over holocausts and sacrifices.
    This adds two important qualifications to the initial answer given by
    Jesus. First, the phrase "and besides him there is no other," borrowed
    from Isaiah 45:21, clears up any further question concerning God's na-
    tionalistic or universal nature. The God of Israel is the one and only
    God. What repercussions such a claim might have on the practice of
    neighborly love, one can only conjecture. Second, the scribe places him-
    self in a well-known prophetic tradition by promoting the love of God
    and neighbor over Temple worship and rituals. However, it is neither
    clear within the prophetic tradition nor here within this passage how this
    scribe's comment should be understood. Is it a critique of the way wor-
    ship is conducted or is it a "blatant rejection of the Temple system"?

3. *You are not far from the kingdom of God.* What prevents the scribe of
    this text from entering or experiencing God's *basileia*? Unlike the man
    who "had many possessions" (10:21), it is not immediately clear what
    he is still lacking. Recalling Jesus' initial proclamation in Galilee that
    the *basileia* is at hand, this scribe may have begun to turn around and
    believe in the good news proclaimed by Jesus (1:14–15). He may have
    found something in the teaching of Jesus (vv. 28 and 32) that caused
    him to reevaluate his understanding of God. Or, perhaps, he still has
    to witness and react to the upcoming passion and death of Jesus and

to the news of his resurrection. Interpreters continue to debate the status of this scribe and their solutions cover a large spectrum, with minimalist and maximalist readings sharing the field.

Pastoral and homiletical notes

1. *No apologetics.* The combination by Jesus of two commandments (love of God and love of neighbor) that are separated in the biblical tradition should not be used as a "proof-text" for the "uniqueness" of Jesus. It may be more profitable to preach on their interconnectedness in light of the well-known texts of the first letter to John (4:9, 20–21).

2. *Role of worship.* The superiority of love of God and neighbors over rituals and sacrifices is a theme as relevant in today's world as it is in the biblical tradition. This theme may be an opportunity to address questions about Christian identity and practices.

3. *Being a Christian today.* In the multicultural environment we find ourselves today, dialogue with, rather than rejection of, the culture (Canaanite gods) may be a necessary part of our growth as Christian communities. As we discover in today's Gospel, in the eyes of God, love and respect of neighbor are paramount, above all else.

4. *Love of God cannot be coerced.* The demands made on Israel in the book of Deuteronomy are grounded in what the Lord has done on their behalf. Likewise, congregations might be reminded that the commandment to love God and neighbor comes *in response to* God's love for all.

5. *What's in a Creed?* The presence of Israel's creed (the *Shema*) in the first reading provides a good occasion to speak about the role and function of creeds in faith communities. Most faith communities profess a certain creed in relation to their faith and beliefs. These creeds are the tie that binds faith communities together and are deeply held and profoundly felt within these communities. It appears to me that love of God and neighbor asks of us understanding and respect in relation to creeds of all faith communities, not simply our own.

<table>
<tr><td>Roman Catholic L
1 Kings 17:10–16
Mark 12:38–44</td><td>Revised Common L
1 Kings 17:8–16
Mark 12:38–44</td></tr>
</table>

Jesus, the Scribes, and the Poor Widow
(Mark 12:38–44)

On 1 Kings 17:8–16

The importance and the role of the Word of the Lord in Israel's history is made known through the extensive presence of prophets in 1—2 Kings, especially the long cycles of Elijah and Elishah (1 Kgs 17—2 Kgs 9). These prophets, as official guardians of the faith, as "champions" of the Lord's Word, continue the mission of Moses to defend the Covenant and its stipulations among a people and their leaders in constant rebellion against their God. God's direct challenge to the introduction of the fertility god, Baal, in Israel's worship by king Ahab and his foreign wife Jezebel appears in the form of a drought that forces Elijah to seek help, first to the east of the Jordan, then outside of Israel.

Once outside Israel, a foreign widow aids Elijah. What ultimately motivates this foreign widow to help Elijah at the price of her own security and that of her son is not immediately clear. The text speaks of God's power or control over the widow (v. 9), of her knowledge of Israel's God, the Lord (v. 12), of Elijah's call "not to fear" (v. 13), and finally of her trust in the promise from the Lord, the God of Israel. All is well that ends well, but some may question why God, the defender of widows and orphans, would command such a sacrifice from a starving widow and her son!

ON MARK 12:38–44
Context

Today's text concludes a block of controversial stories showing Jesus in conflict or discussion with various representatives of the whole leadership of Israel. More immediately, it follows Jesus' criticism of the scribes' understanding of their own Scriptures (12:35–37). This, in turn, will be followed by the so-called Apocalyptic Discourse, which opens with Jesus' announcement to his disciples of the upcoming destruction of the Temple (13:2).

The lectionary selection consists of two episodes: Jesus' denunciation of the scribes for their ostentatious and hypocritical behavior (vv. 38–40) and the story of the Widow's Mite (vv. 41–44). Though different, the two accounts are connected through the catchword "widow" that appears in both stories. It may be important to note that the critique of the scribes in the first story may impact upon one's reading of the second.

Questions

1. Where does the critique of the scribes by Jesus and the episode with the widow take place? What do you think this location represents for the "poor widow"?
2. Can you explain the connection, if any, between these two stories?
3. How do you understand the words of Jesus in verses 43–44, as a praise of the widow or a lament over what she is expected to do?

❧ ❦ ❧

4. Why do you think the scribes will be subjected to the "greater condemnation" (v. 40)?
5. Does the more common translation that the widow put "all she had to live on" say something different about the widow than the more literal translation that she put "her whole life"?
6. What do you think Mark is trying to teach through the story of the Widow's Mite?
7. Do you see a potential danger in Jesus' stereotypical characterization of all scribes?

Interpretive points

1. *Praise or lament?* Traditionally, the widow's attitude has been interpreted as an example of self-sacrificing generosity, singled out by Jesus as an example for the disciples to follow. Seen through a different lens, however, this story may also be interpreted as a lament by Jesus on the part of the "poor widow" because of the demands placed on her by a corrupt religious system (Wright). Mark locates this episode in the Temple area and in the narrative has it follow immediately upon Jesus' indictment of the scribes for "devouring widows' houses." The fact that this episode occurs in the Temple, already condemned by Jesus, coupled with its narrative location in Mark, would appear to favor an interpretation different from its more standard interpretation.

2. *Giving her whole life?* Those favoring this translation like to point out that the generosity of this widow harks back to what Jesus has already said about his own mission (10:43–45) and exemplifies Jesus' offering of his "whole life," an offering that the disciples also made when they "left everything and followed Jesus" (10:28). This offering, to dedicate their lives to the God of Jesus, to bring about the justice proclaimed by him, will come at a high cost, not yet fully understood by the disciples. Jesus, fully understanding the cost, through the action of the widow, attempts once again to convey understanding to the disciples of what their commitment entails. Unlike the rich man who cannot bring himself to give up his wealth (10:21), the widow gives "all that she has to live on."

3. *Avoid stereotyping.* Because of the positive portrayal of the scribe in the previous story, we can deduce that Jesus' indictment here does not cover all scribes. Nevertheless, as a group, they appear in a bad light throughout the Gospel of Mark. Mainline Christian Churches of today reject this stereotyping and encourage Christians to be more understanding and respectful of the Jewish faith tradition.

Pastoral and homiletical notes

1. *Subverting the story?* Although the interpretation of the Widow's Mite story in terms of a lament may make some preachers uncomfortable, the issue raised by such a reading should not be discarded too quickly. It could be an occasion to reflect with the congregation around what the institutional Church requires of them and of what they themselves are prepared to give and why they do so.

2. *A sadistic God?* It will be observed that the story of the widow of Zarephath (first reading) also lends itself to being interpreted as a lament. A starving widow is asked to give up the last bite of food she has for her and for her starving child. One may wonder the image of God this sort of interpretation leaves one with.

3. *Being proactive.* Jesus' indictment of the scribes, as a group, may lend itself to anti-Semitism. Jesus' indictment, however, can also be applied to any hierarchical organization, our Church included, that places power and prestige over the well-being of people. Considering this, and recalling Jesus' earlier denunciation in this Gospel of his disciples' yearning for power, status, and prestige, might prove a good antidote to an anti-Jewish reading of this text.

34A. THIRTY-THIRD SUNDAY IN ORDINARY TIME
Year B

Roman Catholic L
Daniel 12:1–3
Mark 13:24–32

JESUS' TESTAMENT TO THE COMMUNITY
(MARK 13:24–32)

ON DANIEL 12:1–3

Although narratively located during the Exile, the book of Daniel was written in the second century BCE during the Maccabean revolt. One purpose of this book was to encourage people to resist, even to the death, the hellenization plan of the Greek ruler, Archelaus Epiphanus IV. In order to achieve this purpose, the author first presents the heroic examples of the faithful Jews, Daniel and his companions (1—6). Second, he depicts four visions of God's control and final triumph over evil powers, and the vindication of all those who have participated and still participate in the struggle against hellenization (7—12).

Daniel 12:1–4 introduces the concluding part of the fourth and last apocalyptic vision that begins in 10:1. The appearance of the angel Michael—protector of God's people—will mark the beginning of the end time. This final vision of the prophet reveals that, following these distressful times, those who have died, defending their faith over against the temptations of foreign powers, will finally be delivered and vindicated by way of their resurrection from the dead. Without such vindication, the triumph of God's justice and righteousness would be incomprehensible and found wanting.

On Mark 13:24–32
Context

Mark 13 is not, despite appearances, about the end time, but rather about the time of Mark's community. Resorting to a literary genre developed to encourage people in times of trials and persecution, Mark uses apocalyptic imagery to speak of hope and courage to a community seemingly undergoing persecution. These trying times are described in verses 9–13 as well as in 14–20, which may be a reference to the dramatic events of the first Jewish rebellion, ending with the destruction of Jerusalem and its Temple in 70 CE. During these times, a warning is issued to the community not to be led astray by false readings or interpretations of "these things" (vv. 21–23). Those who will stay alert and show perseverance to the end, the elect, will be vindicated when, following some cosmic disruption, the Son of Man riding the clouds, appears with great power and glory (v. 26).

Questions

1. Where would you locate the primary focus of Mark 13, in the future of the disciples or the "end time"?
2. What is your reading or interpretation of verses 24–27, in particular the "coming of the Son of Man"?
3. What lesson do you think the disciples (and readers) can learn from the fig tree?

4. Are your Bible references of any help for interpreting the cosmic images or signs spoken of in verses 24–25?
5. What do you think is the narrative purpose or function of verses 24–27, in particular verses 26–27?
6. How can one reconcile verse 30 with verse 10 and verses 32–37?

Interpretive points

1. *Exegetical and hermeneutical questions.* Mark 13:24–32 raises exegetical and hermeneutical questions not easily ignored. First, what are we to make of the "cosmic signs" that are supposed to precede the coming of the Son of Man in power and glory (vv. 24–27)? To look to these signs, as many

still do today, for information about the end time may be to miss the thrust of the entire apocalyptic discourse, most especially verses 24–27. As was noted in some previous comments on the apocalyptic literature, the primary purpose of Mark 13 is not to inform readers about the end of this world, but rather to provide information on how to live in this interim time that precedes the end. The description of this interim time in terms of trials and persecutions is not, however, very appealing. Why would people face opposition, trials, even death for the sake of the Gospel? The answer, as in Daniel, appears to lie in some future vindication. This vindication is presented as a vision of the return of the Son of Man in glory and power to gather the faithful ones (13:26). Without this vision, the frequent appeals to vigilance and watchfulness that are found in the passage might appear groundless. To the contrary, this vision will strengthen the disciples and the community and help them face "even death for the sake of the Gospel."

2. *Waiting for the* parousia. The statement of Jesus that "this generation will not pass away until all these things have taken place" (v. 30) is generally understood as a reference to an imminent *parousia*. Such a statement may, in this context, appear to strengthen Jesus' call for watchfulness to the disciples (vv. 33–36). What, one may ask however, is its relevancy for readers of today who know that the return of the Son of Man still lies in an unknown future? This "vindication" does not appear to be sufficient motivation, today, for a life of commitment to the Gospel. Mark provides us only with Jesus' promise to his disciples that he will go before them to Galilee (14:28; 16:7). This "meeting in Galilee" will tell the disciples that despite their failures, including their total collapse during the passion, Jesus will not abandon them. Mark 13 does not promise an easy future for the disciples. They will need understanding, discernment, patience, courage, and above all faith in the presence of Jesus among them.

3. *Beware of becoming oppressors.* Apocalyptic literature is a literature of resistance that runs the risk of becoming texts of oppression (Sharon Ringe). Powerful insiders, the "elect" who interpret such texts, hold the potential to define and dominate a community. What then, one may ask, happens to the "non-elect," those whom the dominant in-

siders may name as outsiders? These texts of resistance were primarily written for marginalized, powerless outsiders, but can be easily appropriated by the powerful and turned against the very people they were written to help. It may, therefore, be appropriate to question whether people who are not marginalized and powerless can genuinely read and justly interpret such texts.

Pastoral and homiletical notes

1. *A more suitable passage.* In both lectionaries, the Gospel reading for this Sunday is drawn from Mark 13, but the passages are different. Because of its focus on the end time, the selection from the *Roman Catholic Lectionary* (13:24–32) appears to be more relevant to the liturgical context than Mark 13:1–8.

2. *The medium is not the message.* Because of its focus on the end time, many preachers dread preaching on this Sunday. They know all too well the rather enigmatic chapter 13 of Mark or its equivalent in Matthew and Luke. By way of introduction, they may want to explain to their congregations why Mark has chosen the apocalyptic imagery or language to address a very special situation of his community. In this case, the medium might not be, as it were, the message.

3. *Translating the message for today.* The narrative and theological function of Mark 13:24–32 is not without pastoral implications. How, for example, can the vision of a "return" of the Son of Man in glory and power challenge and encourage today's congregations to live up to their Christian commitments? One particularly tough challenge for preachers on this day may be to separate the eschatological dimension of the passage from its apocalyptic presentation. Another challenge may be to ask what, if not always opposition, persecution, and trials, are the "signs" that will accompany today's proclamation of the Gospel?

4. *Connecting the two readings.* God's vindication of the "faithful ones" is the theme that connects both first and third readings on this Sunday.

Revised Common L
Daniel 12:1–3
Mark 13:1–8

Looking beyond the Temple . . .
(Mark 13:1–8)

On Daniel 12:1–3

For the study guide on Daniel 12:1–3, see chapter 34a.

On Mark 13:1–8
Context

The notice that Jesus is leaving the Temple (13:1) serves to remind readers of the events that have just taken place in this key location. As already noted, Mark 11—12 presents Jesus in conflict, successful conflict, with various segments of the Jewish leadership. On the day following his cleansing action, Jesus returned to the Temple area. It is here that these conflicts or confrontations took place. As Jesus is leaving the Temple, a nameless disciple draws his attention to the colossal size of its buildings. Jesus' prediction of their total destruction confirms what has already transpired in the previous two chapters, the end of the Temple (11:12–24). The next scene has Jesus sitting on the Mount of Olives, opposite the Temple and, not surprisingly, moving quickly beyond its horizon.

Questions

1. Why do you think Mark 13 is often referred to as the apocalyptic discourse?
2. What event or events do you think the two questions from the disciples are referring to?
3. Does the text provide any criteria for identifying the false voices and the false prophets?

⊷ ❀ ❀ ⊷

4. Can you recall ancient prophets who proclaimed the end of the first Temple due to Israel's apostasy?
5. "[They] asked him privately" (13:3). Where before in Mark has the pattern or model of public/private teaching been used?
6. What situation do you think Jesus is addressing in 13:5–9, the context of Mark's community or the eschatological future?
7. What do you think is the narrative function of the entire discourse (Mark 13) within, and at this particular place in, the Gospel narrative?

Interpretive points

1. *A pause in the narrative.* Mark 13 interrupts the narrative flow. Indeed, Jesus' confrontation with the authorities (Mark 11—12) would be a more suitable preparation for the final confrontation that is about to take place in the passion (Mark 14—15). Mark's second lengthy discourse (for the first, see Mark 4) compels readers to pause, so to speak; it brings them to a halt in order to hear Jesus addressing "in private" those first disciples whom he has called to follow him (1:16–20).

2. *Mark and the apocalyptic genre.* Mark 13 is most often referred to as an apocalyptic discourse (of which we find parallel versions in Matthew and Luke), or the Little Apocalypse. Apocalypses are a very particular literature that developed in full force in the centuries around the Current Era. The book of Daniel and the book of Revelation are probably the best-known canonical examples of this type of literature. The word "apocalypse" comes from the Greek *apokalypsis*, meaning "revelation." This revelation looks to the future, the end time, just as does eschatology (the study of the last things). But, in contrast with the latter, apocalyptic writ-

ings speak about the end, God's final act in history, in a more descriptive, graphic, and explosive way. It is therefore correct to say that the term "apocalyptic" describes both a type of literature and a new way to speak about the end time. It also accounts for the fact that if all apocalypses are, of necessity, eschatological, not all eschatology is apocalyptic!

One important characteristic of apocalyptic literature is its development in the midst of, and for, communities undergoing persecution. Contrary to popular views, it was not its purpose to put fear in people, but to bring them hope in the midst of their trials and difficulties. How this was done varies with each author. Because of the way Mark 13 is construed, it will be useful to recall here the strategy used in the book of Daniel. The author of this prophetic book writes in the second century BCE, but actually speaks as if he were living in the time of the Babylonian king, Nebuchadnezzar, some 400 years earlier. What then appears like "prophecies" are in fact flashbacks of the respective falls of the Babylonian, Persian, and Greek empires! Through such a device, the author hopes to convince people that a similar fate is awaiting the present Greek leadership of Antiochus IV. Likewise in Mark 13, events that the community may be experiencing or have already experienced, such as persecution and the destruction of Jerusalem and its Temple, are presented as "prophecies" from Jesus, just before he enters his passion. Some of these events may be already in the past, but, narratively, they are yet to come.

3. *Is Mark an apocalypse?* Strictly speaking, Mark 13 is not an apocalypse, but it includes apocalyptic traits that account for the way this chapter of Mark is still designated today. More importantly, it provides little, if any, information about the end of the world. Note how cryptic the discourse becomes when it moves beyond the time of Mark's community, as here in 13:7–8, and still more clearly in verses 24–32. "This is but the beginning of the birth pangs" (v. 8) and "But about that day or hour no one knows, neither the angels in heaven, nor the Son, but only the Father" (v. 32). Although Mark uses here images of the "end of the world," he is ultimately concerned about the future of the community. It is to that very community, victim in all likelihood of persecution, that the following words of Jesus are addressed: "Let the reader understand" (v. 14) and "What I say to you, I say to

all" (v. 37). One can think of Mark 13 as Jesus' last testament to the Markan community, a "farewell discourse" in which he instructs them how to live after his passion, death, and resurrection. It is up to the reader or interpreter to find out what he wants us to understand.

4. *"Beware that no one leads you astray" (v. 5).* When "these things" happen (wars, conflicts, earthquakes, and whatever the "desolating sacrilege" may point to), voices will be heard giving interpretations of these events. Many will claim to be messiahs and purport to have "the" truth. Jesus' warning not to be deceived by such claims begs the question: How is one to determine or discern these things? The text provides at least three criteria. First, these things are not "signs" that the end is near, "but the beginning of the birth pangs" (v. 8). Second, the end will not take place before the good news has been proclaimed to all nations (v. 10). Third and lastly, what will ultimately identify true disciples or evangelizers is, as is about to happen to Jesus, suffering and persecution not "signs and wonders" (v. 22).

5. *"Do not be alarmed" (v. 7).* Suffering, opposition, and persecutions are not to be interpreted as signs of the end of the world. Rather, they are the conditions or consequences of the struggle between the forces of evil and the preaching of the Gospel. Just as Jesus has encountered opposition, rejection and, ultimately, death in his commitment to proclaiming the upcoming *basileia* of God, so will the community in the fulfillment of their mission to all nations in Jesus' name (13:10). In this regard, why, one may ask, were verses 9–13 left out from today's reading? They form the core of the whole discourse, speaking to the travails that the community is experiencing in the midst of the world. (Not surprisingly, Matthew deleted these words from his version of the apocalyptic or eschatological discourse [Matt 24] and appended them to the missionary instructions that Jesus gives to the Twelve in 10:17–21.)

Pastoral and homiletical notes

1. *Debunking the apocalypse!* The Gospel reading for the last Sunday in Ordinary time comes from Mark 13 in both lectionaries, but the se-

lections are different. Whatever the rationale behind the choice of Mark 13:1–8, it may be an occasion to debunk certain popular misinterpretations about this chapter.

2. *It's about the community!* On this Sunday, preachers have little choice but to introduce their congregations to Mark's use of apocalyptic to address the situation of his community. The interpretation offered above may go a long way towards, not only eliminating the speculations and fear created over time by these apocalyptic images, but also helping congregations to hear a message concerning life in their community.

3. *Returning to Galilee?* It has not escaped biblical interpreters that Mark 13 was Mark's way of modeling the life of his community on that of Jesus. Its location just before the narrative of the passion, death, and resurrection of Jesus is a clear invitation to see in this chapter more than simply what a scholar has called "the passion of Mark's community." The good news must first be proclaimed to all nations before the "return" of the Son of Man. This assertion of Mark leaves open the question of when the community or the readers will experience their vindication. The answer may lie in the final words of Jesus in the Gospel that he will meet them once again in Galilee (16:7), the very area where Jesus' ministry first began.

SOLEMNITIES OF THE LORD IN ORDINARY TIME

The *Roman Catholic Lectionary* includes three Solemnities of the Lord during Ordinary Time: Trinity Sunday (common to both lectionaries), the Body and Blood of Christ, and the Sacred Heart of Jesus. In the year of Mark, it is only the feast of the Body and Blood of Christ that includes a reading from Mark's Gospel.

Also included here, for convenience sake, is the feast of the Transfiguration of Our Lord. Though not explicitly identified in the Sacramentary as a solemnity of the Lord, it functions as such for all purposes, as it replaces in the *Roman Catholic Lectionary* one Sunday in Ordinary Time in the summer.

35. Most Holy Body and Blood of Christ (Corpus Christi)

Year B

Roman Catholic L
Exodus 24:3–8
Mark 14:12–16, 22–26

Jesus' Last Passover Meal with his Disciples
(Mark 14:12–16, 22–26)

On Exodus 24:3–8

Exodus 19—24 recounts the covenant that God struck with the people of Israel at the foot of Mount Sinai. This covenant shaped Israel's identity as God's people and these five chapters have been called, not surprisingly, the Mission Statement of Israel. Exodus 19 announces the divine covenant and the people's readiness to obey the "words" of the Lord. This is followed in chapters 21—23 by the proclamation of these words (or the Law), often referred to as the Covenant Code. The covenant is then ratified in Exodus 24, with two solemn rituals: the sprinkling of blood (vv. 3–8) and the meal (vv. 9–11).

Today's reading describes the first of these rituals, the ritual of blood (vv. 3–8). By sprinkling the animal blood on both the altar (v. 6) and the people (v. 8), Moses ties the two parties together. The ceremony, coupled with the people's promise to obey the Lord's words, seals the covenant or the relationship between God and the people. Yet, as the book of Exodus will reveal, the "real" covenant between the two parties occurs some 10 chapters further (Exod 34), following the "sin" of the people with the golden calf (Exod 32:1–6). This is where God finally agrees to "renew" the covenant, not this time with a people who promise full obedience, but with a "stiff-necked people" who will need to be shown constant mercy and pardon (Exod 34:9–29).

On Mark 14:12–16, 22–26
Context

Jesus' last meal with the disciples (14:12–14, 22–26) is one of the preparatory scenes leading to the passion narrative. It is preceded by a prelude (14:1–2), the anointing of Jesus by an unknown woman (vv. 3–9), and the betrayal of Judas (10—11). It is followed by Jesus' prediction of the failure of his friends, including the betrayal of Judas (vv. 15–21), and their withdrawal to Gethsemane (vv. 32–42).

Questions

1. Why do you think Mark sets the last meal of Jesus in the context of the Jewish Passover (v. 12)?
2. What do you think the instructions given to the disciples, here and in Mark 11:1–7 are meant to convey to the reader?
3. How does the language of the Last Supper narrative echo the feeding stories (Mark 6 and 8), and what can it tell us of the relationship between the two?

✥ ✦ ✦ ✥

4. How are the following biblical texts: Exodus 24:3–8; Isaiah 53:11–12; and Mark 10:45, used by the author to interpret the upcoming death of Jesus?
5. Why do you think we should hesitate to speak of this passage in terms of Jesus' *institution* of the Eucharist? A comparison with 1 Corinthians 11 and Luke 24 might help to answer this question.
6. What distinguishes this covenant from the covenant made with Israel at the Sinai, and where is the potential danger for supersessionism?
7. What does Jesus' reference to the new *basileia* of God (v. 25) say about the significance of this last meal?

Interpretive points

1. *A Passover meal.* The well-known contrast between the Synoptic presentation of Jesus' last meal as a "Passover meal" and John's presentation of the meal occurring the day before Passover has given rise to much historical discussion over the actual dating of that supper. Did

it occur on the evening of the regular Passover meal as in the Synoptic Gospels, or, as in John, on the night before the Passover lambs were killed (13:1; 18:28; 19:14)? Scholars have generally preferred the Johannine dating, while agreeing that this was still a Passover meal. However captivating this historical question may be, it should not obscure the fact that in Mark, as in the other two Synoptic Gospels, Jesus' last meal with his disciples is clearly, albeit quite differently, a Passover meal (14:12, 14, 16).

2. *The Christian covenant.* Although a Passover meal, Jesus' last meal with his disciples differs in that it takes on a more personal dimension. Following the announcement of his betrayal by one of the Twelve (vv. 17–21), Jesus is said to proceed with a double symbolic action over a loaf of bread and a cup of wine. Using words reminiscent of his actions earlier on when he fed 5000 and 4000 people, he takes the bread, and after a blessing, breaks it, and gives it to his disciples, saying: "take, this is my body" ("which is given for you" in Luke 22:19 and "that is for you" in 1 Corinthians 11:24). He then takes the cup, and after giving thanks, gives it to all of them to drink, saying, "This is the blood of the covenant, which is poured out for many. (Both Paul and Luke has "This cup . . . is the new covenant in my blood".) These words and actions over the bread and the cup have been understood in light of Jesus' upcoming death. Likewise, earlier on, Jesus had interpreted the action of a woman, anointing "[his] body beforehand for its burial" (14:8). Recognizable echoes of Mark 10:45, of Exodus 24:3–8, and possibly also of Isaiah 53:11–12 corroborate such an interpretation. Exodus 24:3–8 is particularly significant. Just as the Sinai covenant was sealed with a blood sacrifice, with blood sprinkled upon the altar and the people, so is this covenant being established by Jesus' blood, to be shared by many. Unlike Paul and Luke, however, Mark, according to the best manuscript reading, does not explicitly speak of a "new" covenant, but only of "the blood of the covenant."

3. *From tragedy to Gospel.* As an interpretive event of the death and resurrection of Jesus, the Last Supper, not unlike the anointing of Jesus by an unknown woman (14:3–9), transforms "what would have been a tragedy of Jesus into the Gospel of Jesus" (LaVerdiere).

4. *The Lord's Supper?* Mark may have known of the liturgical celebration of the Eucharist or the Lord's Supper, as described in 1 Corinthians 11, but, it clearly is not the focus of his account. In this respect, editors of some bibles may be misleading readers in using such headings as "Institution of the Lord's Supper" or simply "The Lord's Supper."

Pastoral and homiletical notes

1. *Preaching about the Lord's Supper.* Admittedly, it may prove difficult not to speak of the Eucharist or the Lord's Supper on this day. Nevertheless, preachers should be aware that what today's Gospel reading points to is, not the Eucharist, but the sacrificial death of Jesus, symbolized in the broken bread and his shared blood for the sake of many. True, this symbolism is at the heart of the Lord's Supper, but to bring the Eucharist into focus they will have to reach beyond Mark's description of Jesus' last Passover meal to the Lord's Supper as described primarily in 1 Corinthians 11 and, in less clear terms, in Luke 24.

2. *The (new) covenant in Christ.* Traditionally, Jesus' words over the cup, especially in their Pauline and Lucan versions, have been understood as inaugurating a *new* covenant in the blood of Christ, in fulfillment of the prophecy of Jeremiah (31:31; see also Ezek 36). Over the centuries, many Christians have believed this "new" covenant in Christ had actually replaced the original divine covenant made with the people of Israel at the foot of Mount Sinai (Exod 24:3–12). In the aftermath of the *Shoah*, all mainline Christian Churches have now rejected such teaching. As Paul says in Romans 11, God's covenant with Israel has never been abrogated or revoked. This "new" teaching and understanding of the relationship of the Jewish people to their God continue to generate serious theological reflections and discussions. In light of this new reality, how should Christians today understand Judaism and the Jewish people? At present, the thesis that Jesus has through his death "fulfilled" the original covenant appears to be the most common way for Christians to speak of what has happened "in Christ."

3. *What about Hebrews?* Today's second reading from Hebrews appears to support the idea that the new covenant in Christ has "replaced" or

superseded the covenant made with the Jewish people. In the previous chapter, the author of Hebrews has made clear what this "new covenant" in Christ actually meant for the original one. "In speaking of 'a new covenant,' he has made the first one obsolete. And what is obsolete and growing old will soon disappear" (8:13). This view contrasts Paul's own understanding, which is being reclaimed today by all mainline Christian Churches. Such a contrast speaks loud and clear to the difficult task awaiting theologians of rethinking our Christian theology with a view to reflect this new understanding of the relations between Christians and the Jewish people. In this respect, the passage from Hebrews will not be of much help to preachers who may wish, on this festive day, to speak about this "new covenant" in Christ, without denigrating one of the most revered markers of Jewish identity, their covenant with God. To be aware of the dangers inherent to this crucial Christian teaching will go a long way towards preaching in a way that will be both empowering to Christians and respectful of Judaism and other faiths.

Roman Catholic L
Daniel 7:9–10, 13–14
Mark 9:2–10

AND HE WAS TRANSFIGURED
BEFORE THEM
(MARK 9:2–10)

ON DANIEL 7:9–10, 13–14

As the first of four apocalyptic visions, Daniel 7 is usually seen as the heart of the book of Daniel (for a brief outline of the book, see chapter 5 on the Second Sunday of Lent). There is an obvious connection between the prophet's first vision (7:2–8) and the Babylonian king's dream in chapter 2. They both refer to the four beasts representing, in all probability, the empires of the Babylonians, the Medes, the Persians, and the Greeks. More importantly, this chapter forecasts the destruction of these empires, in particular the Greek kingdom and its present ruler, Antiochus Epiphanus IV (9:11–12).

Daniel's vision of the four beasts (vv. 2–8) is followed by a judgment scene, which takes place in heaven in the presence of the Ancient One and his accompanying court (vv. 9–10). The judgment is passed on the horn and the beast. Antiochus IV is to be put to death, bringing his dominion to an end. The judgment on the other beasts, whose lives are momentarily preserved, is that they are to be deprived of their dominion (vv. 11–12). Having taken dominion away from the beasts, the Ancient One gives it to a "one like a human figure coming [to him] with the clouds of heaven " (v. 13). This will be an everlasting dominion and this kingship will be indestructible (v.14). Who this human-like figure might be has been the object of much discussion in scholarship. Today, there is little support for the "traditional opinion" which identified this "heavenly figure" as the Messiah. Such identification owed more to later apocalyptic books such as the first book of Enoch and to the Christian interpretation of Jesus in terms of the danielic Human One. Present-day scholarship favors a symbolic interpretation of this human-like figure, more in line with the symbolic reference of the four beasts. In this interpretation, this human-like figure would stand for "the holy ones of the Most High" (7:18, 22, and 27), the people of Israel under persecution.

ON MARK 9:2–10

For context, questions, and interpretive points concerning this passage, see chapter 5 on the second Sunday in Lent.

Pastoral and homiletical notes

1. *A Sunday celebration.* The feast of the Transfiguration of the Lord, which falls on August 6, will, in both Roman Catholic and Anglican Liturgies, always be celebrated on a Sunday in Ordinary Time (or Proper).

2. *Connection with Daniel 7.* Today's reading from Daniel was not only chosen for its description of the Ancient One in words that are reminiscent of those used for Jesus' transfiguration. In all probability, it was also meant to point to Jesus' frequent use of this human-like figure as a name or title for himself in the Gospels. This very name, Human One or Son of Man, is found in the conclusion of the story of the Transfiguration (Mark 9:9).

3. *Avoiding the supersessionist pitfall.* The above interpretation of the danielic Human One, though a perfectly legitimate Christian reading, should not be understood as being a dismissal of Jewish readings of the same passage. As we have been reminded in the last document from the Pontifical Biblical Commission (*The Jewish People and Their Holy Scriptures in the Christian Bible*, 2001), a Jewish reading is as legitimate and valid as the Christian one.

4. *With the disciples in view.* Although the feast of the Transfiguration is a feast of our *Lord* Jesus, preachers will do well to remember that the primary focus of Mark's account of this episode is on the three disciples. This episode has, in Mark, a specific function in the journey of Jesus and his disciples towards Jerusalem. Perhaps our reflection for today should also be more focused on our journey and the issues that this passage may raise for us.